THE FORGOTTEN NAVY

tten Navy

JOHN STOCKTON

INTERVIEW
You ™

Published by Interview You
Athens, GA
www.interviewyou.net

ISBN 0-9773365-0-6

Printed in the United States of America

To Dad, in appreciation for all you have done
for your family, your fellow servicemen,
and your country. We love you.

Pat and Ron

The Forgotten Navy

JOHN STOCKTON

In 1943, at the age of 18, John Stockton enlisted in the United States Navy. After completing boot camp at Newport, Rhode Island, he was sent to Armed Guard School in Little Creek, Virginia, where he was formally assigned to the U.S. Naval Armed Guard.

The story of the armed guard is an interesting one. At the beginning of World War II, American merchant ships were unarmed, in compliance with the Neutrality Act of 1936. They were easy prey to German aircraft and submarines, and a number of them were sunk. On November 17, 1941, Congress repealed the section of the Neutrality Act that prevented arming merchant ships. Soon afterwards the merchant ships were armed, and the armed guard was established, as it had been in WWI, to provide trained naval gunners to serve aboard these ships.

After completing Armed Guard School in Virginia, Stockton reported to the Armed Guard Center in Brooklyn, New York, where he was assigned to his first ship, the tanker SS *Esso Dover*. Owned by the Standard Oil Company, the ship was launched February 19, 1921 as the *Cerro Ebano*. Around 1940, Standard Oil renamed all the tankers in its fleet with the word *Esso* followed by the name of a city.

Stockton recalls his first voyage aboard the *Esso Dover*,

sailing in convoy from New York to London. He pulls no punches as he tells how he and his fellow armed guard members had received no training for how to fire the ship's largest gun, and how one of the ship's gunners shot down a German bomber by sheer luck. He recounts the ship's arrival in England, his boisterous liberty in London, and how the ship was pummeled by a hurricane on its return voyage to New York.

Stockton's second voyage aboard the *Esso Dover* took him to South America. The ship didn't encounter combat on this voyage, but Stockton's memoirs provide many interesting facts about the ship's itinerary, the ports visited, and the adventures (and misadventures) of the crew.

Upon returning to the U.S. in 1944, Stockton was assigned to his first liberty ship, the SS *Margaret Brent*.

Liberty ships were produced, beginning in 1941, to meet our nation's emergency need for more cargo ships. As the U.S. prepared to enter WWII, it was clear that a large number of merchant ships would need to be built in a hurry. For its basic cargo ship, the U.S. Maritime Commission settled on a modified version of an 1879 British design: a ship 441 feet long, 56 feet wide, and powered by an oil-fired steam engine. These liberty ships could carry over 9,000 tons of cargo (equivalent to 300 railroad freight cars) and had a top speed of 11 knots.

The first 14 liberty ships were launched on September 27, 1941, and the first of these was the SS *Patrick Henry*, launched by President Franklin D. Roosevelt. At the launching, President Roosevelt quoted from Patrick Henry's 1775 "Give me liberty or give me death" speech, and he said that this new class of ships would bring liberty to Europe. From then on, these emergency cargo ships, officially known as type EC2-S-C1, would be called liberty ships.

The liberty ship program was an enormous success: between 1941 and 1945, over 2,700 liberty ships were built at 18 U.S. shipyards. John Stockton would end up serving aboard two of them.

Stockton describes his voyage to Europe aboard the liberty ship *Margaret Brent* as "uneventful," and unfortunately provides few details of it. The voyage was certainly important: the ship's cargo was ammunition needed for the D-Day invasion of Normandy.

Upon returning to the U.S., Stockton was assigned to another liberty ship, the SS *William B. Allison*, in January of 1945. This voyage would turn out to be far from "uneventful": the ship was headed to the South Pacific, the territory of Japanese kamikaze pilots. Indeed, on May 25, 1945, off the southeast coast of Okinawa, the *Allison* was struck by an aerial Japanese torpedo that killed seven crew members and severely damaged the ship.

Stockton's memoirs regarding the *Allison* concentrate on the events that occurred after the ship's arrival at Eniwetok, in the Marshall Islands; they tell very little of the long voyage southward from New York, through the Panama Canal, and across the vast empty miles of the Pacific Ocean.

Fortunately, two of Stockton's shipmates aboard the *Allison* wrote accounts that cover this part of the voyage and sent them to Stockton. One account is by Henry "Hank" Valli, a fellow armed guard who served as gunner's mate second class aboard the *Allison*; the other is by Asa "Ace" Casterlin, a merchant marine who served as the ship's second radio operator. Portions of both accounts have been included in this edition, whenever relevant, to fill in missing parts of the story and to help shed more light on some of Stockton's experiences.

Stockton's final chapters testify to the ironic and unpredictable nature of war. Upon arriving at Eniwetok, Stockton is happy to get to visit his brother Walt, who happens to be there serving aboard the destroyer USS *Ingersoll*. All too soon, however, the *Allison* arrives at Okinawa, where it faces its deadly encounter with the enemy.

Throughout his memoirs, Stockton is refreshingly candid: training was not always adequate; officers were not always competent; and, for better or worse, men would be men. But there is also a pride in his voice, the hard-earned pride of a veteran. And, perhaps above all, there is his hope and concern that the armed guard not be forgotten.

In 1946, the Office of the Chief of Naval Operations published a study of the armed guard's role in WWII. This study gives high praise to the armed guard:

> The defense of merchant ships by the Armed Guard of the United States Navy . . . is as thrilling a story of triumph over difficulties, of heroism, devotion to

duty, sacrifice, and courage as exists in the annals of the nation. This story, which for reasons of military security was veiled in secrecy during the war, deserves to be told.

We are proud to help John Stockton tell his part of this story.

Editor, INTERVIEW YOU

PREFACE

What prompted me to write about my experiences in the armed guard was when, in a group of veterans and non-veterans, I was asked what branch of the service I had served in. I said, "The armed guard." No one in the group had ever heard of it. They thought it was an honor guard that carried the flags in parades, or a group that stood guard over monuments. It almost made me cry.

That is why I am calling my WWII memoirs *The Forgotten Navy*. The armed guard part of the navy – gunners aboard merchant ships in WWI and WWII – needs to be remembered.

Many men in the navy and merchant marine lost their lives or were maimed for life. Many members of the armed guard had a worse time than I did. I consider myself lucky compared to other shipmates I have had the privilege to sail with.

The following is my true story of my service in the armed guard. It is so good to be remembered, and I hope that my story will help people remember the armed guard.

John Stockton

C H A P T E R   1

ENLISTMENT AND TRAINING

CHAPTER 1

First, I would like to tell you how I ended up in the armed
guard. It all started when I turned 18, just out of high school.
One day in 1943 some friends and I were all standing on
the street corner in Rockaway, New Jersey. We wondered
what we should do, get jobs or join the navy. There were
five of us, all fresh from high school. We decided to join the
navy.

After we enlisted we all had to report to Newark, New
Jersey, for our physicals. Nick Nito and I passed and were
taken.

We were to report to the Navy Induction Center in Newark,
New Jersey. We had to take another physical – I guess to
prove we were alive. The first order was to remove all your
clothes. Just think how you feel undressing in front of
about 50 other men, standing there stark naked with all of
us looking to see how well each of us were endowed.

Then we heard our second command: "Pull her back, milk
her down, piss in the bucket, and walk around. Next."
Really, they gave us a paper cup. Then came the rest of the
physical. We were then told to line up in alphabetical order.

You never saw such a mess. They kept asking you what your last name is. I thought the navy knew all our names and could have called our names.

We were then sent by train to boot camp in Newport, Rhode Island. It seems every time I went from one place to another it was always at night. We arrived about 1 a.m. It had been a long day.

We were given cots in barracks C for the night. I was assigned to barracks C, hammock # 128, third floor. In WWI my father was in the same barracks, same floor, hammock # 129. I was in Company 396; in WWI my father was in Company 395.

What I can remember of boot camp is how proud I felt to be a part of the navy on Saturdays for captains' inspections and the parade that followed. It brought goose bumps to my body. Another thing I remember is when I fell asleep in seamanship class and, when awakened by the instructor, had to stand up and hold a link of anchor chain for over one hour. Try this one time and you will never fall asleep again in any class. One other thing is when we went to muster under a 5"/38 gun and the gunners above did not know we were there and fired off a round. We couldn't hear for two days because of the tremendous noise of the explosion in the confined quarters where we were. I feel that this is where I lost most of my hearing in my left ear.

We were given tests to see what we were suited for in the navy. I always wanted to be an electrician, and Nick wanted to be a plumber. Both of us passed the tests and were assigned to go to further schooling after boot camp. At least that is what we thought. We were supposed to be in boot camp for nine weeks. After five weeks of boot training we were awakened at 3 a.m. and told to get all of our gear together and be at muster at 5 a.m. We didn't know what was going on. We were never told that there were school teachers, college graduates, and other professionals in Companies 396, 397, and 398 (a total of 320 men). It didn't matter where you were supposed to go; we were all "selected volunteers."

We were taken via train and then by ferry to Armed Guard School in Little Creek, Virginia. This was my second station in the U.S. There, we were told that we had just volunteered for the armed guard. At the first muster we were told they needed mess cooks for two weeks. That was how long we were to be there. Again, they wanted "volunteers." All men whose last name started from "A" to "O" were going to school; all others were mess cooks. You guessed it – I had just "volunteered" again.

We were taken to our new lodgings, a long narrow building about 100 feet long with so much mud on the wooden floor that you could almost scrape it off with a shovel. (It had rained for the past week.) We didn't complain because we did not want to "volunteer" again. We all knew it was only for two weeks. We could survive that. We were told it was only two weeks, but it ended up being four weeks. Never believe what they tell you when you first join the navy. We all survived the mess duty and finally got two weeks of training about how to load the guns and identify enemy aircraft. After that, I never saw Nick again until after the war was over.

CHAPTER 2

THE SS *Esso Dover*

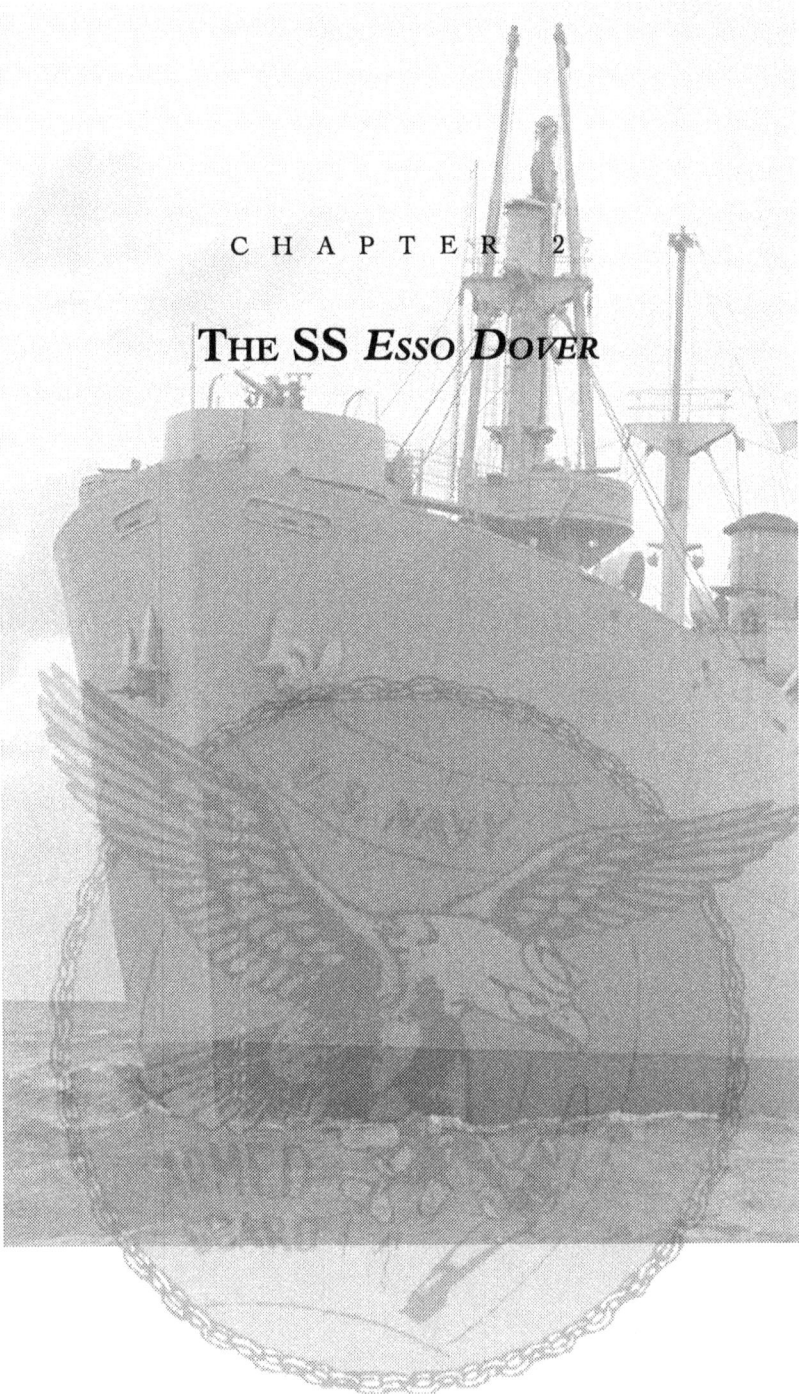

CHAPTER 2

We were then sent to the Brooklyn Armed Guard Center in New York, again by train. The only time we saw water was on the ferry. When we arrived at the center we were issued foul-weather gear, which meant North Atlantic duty. We learned fast. It was now 13 weeks in the navy. We were told we were being assigned to a ship, so we should wait on the bridge, a makeshift row of benches in a balcony. After about three hours of sitting I heard my name called, and I was told to muster in front of the foul-weather gear supply department. This is where I first met my new shipmates: seven seaman 2/C, one gunnery officer, one gunner's mate 2/C, one signalman 3/C. For those who don't know what "C" means, it is "class," as in first class, second class, and third class.

Now it was finally time to board the ship. We were at Pier 92 in New York, and the Red Cross passed out coffee and doughnuts, and also a small ditty bag with toiletries in it. Then we went to a small trailer with cigarettes in it, where a Red Cross lady handed out cigarettes. I said, "I don't smoke," and the lady said, "You will before this war is over." And I did. Today, both the Red Cross and the government say I can't smoke.

With my newfound wealth, we proceeded to go aboard ship. I had never seen as big a ship as was in front of me now – a new liberty ship. I thought, "Boy, this will be nice to live on her." Wrong. We went up to the gangway across the deck and down another to a waiting whale boat and a small barge aft of it. We were told to put our gear on the barge and get in the whale boat. We left the beautiful liberty and passed under the George Washington Bridge. It was now dark and we were still going out in the bay. Finally we came up on the oldest ship I had ever seen, an old tanker, the SS *Esso Dover*. We hesitated a minute, but the officer said to get aboard. We all got aboard and the whaleboat left. We were then taken to our new quarters, all the way aft under a large gun deck (although we didn't know it was a gun deck until morning).

I finally learned some navy talk, and we were underway 15 minutes after we got aboard. There was no chance to see the gun; we were told to muster at the bridge. I can't remember the captain's name, but I do remember what he said. He was very blunt, so good that he scared the devil out of us, including our gunnery officer, who had been in the navy about as long as we had. The captain said we have no fire and boat drills aboard this ship. He said that we are sitting on top of about 100 thousand gallons of aviation fuel. "If we are hit, you won't need a life jacket, just a parachute." That was the end of his talk, short and sweet.

CHAPTER 3

THE SHIP'S GUNS

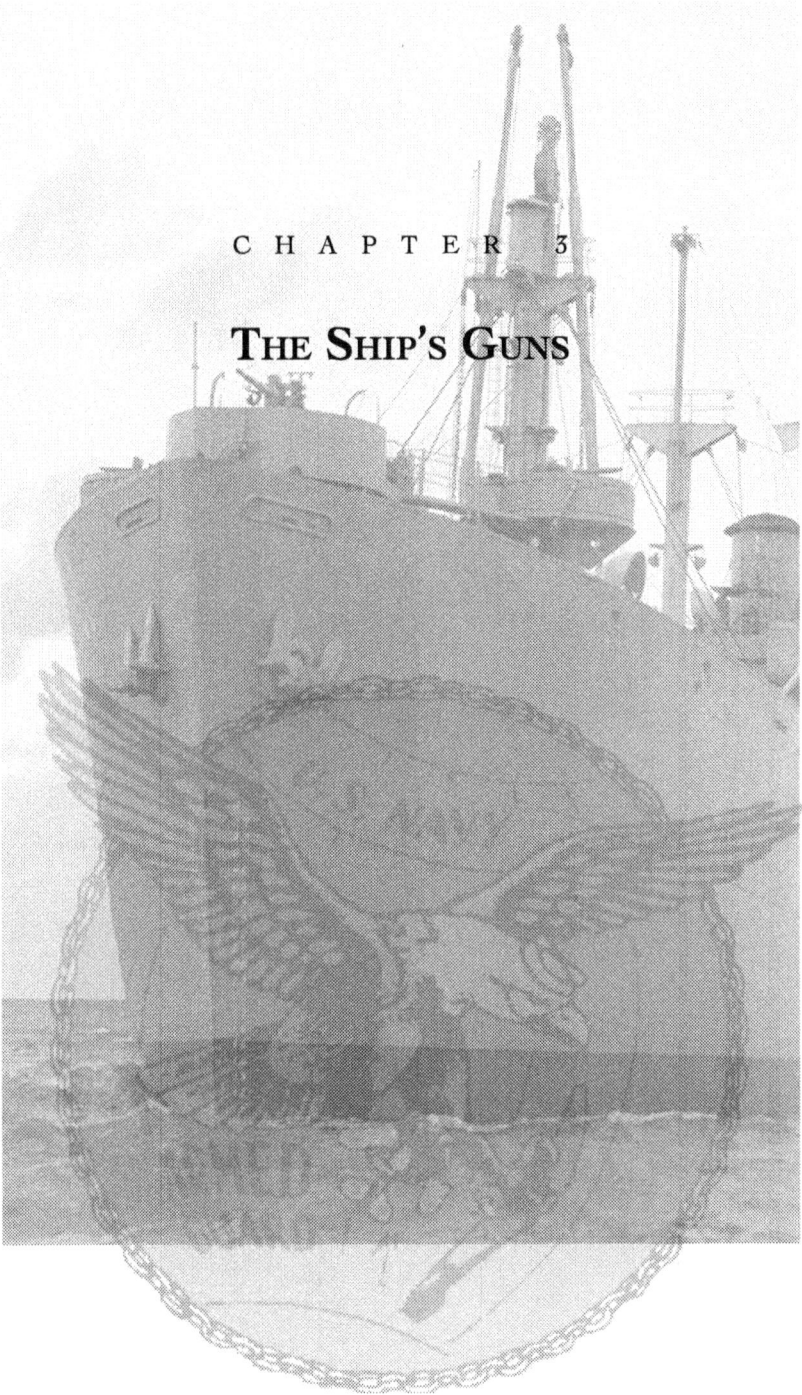

CHAPTER 3

It was now September of 1943. I had been in the navy for
13 weeks, and we were 50 miles at sea. We went to look at
the aft gun we were living under. It was called a 5"/51, an
old battleship gun. It had been reconditioned and looked
very good. The only catch was we had never had any training for this gun. After reading the manual, we finally mas-
tered how to load and fire it, but not at the present time.

Within our convoy, our ship sailed in what was called "coffin corner," which was way back of the rest of the convoy.
In case we got hit by a torpedo, we would not blow other
ships up.

We had silk powder bags and five-inch projectiles. The gunnery officer got permission from the captain to fire the gun.
They had a destroyer escort drop a large balloon over for
us to see if we could hit it. That was the first mistake. We
had drilled on the gun for two days. We loaded it and got
the ok to fire. On the first and only firing, we went through
the drills like old salts, and then we fired the gun. We never
hit the balloon, but we did a lot of damage to our own ship
and our quarters. We had an old cane chair in the entrance
to our quarters; the blast picked up the chair and blew the

cane bottom clear out of it. All we saw was the flash of the explosion at the end of the barrel. Down below our quarters was the galley. All the pots and pans were knocked off their hangers and the plates came down, which caused a lot to break. The galley was a mess. Two fire extinguishers also came off their hangers and went off, shooting foam all over our quarters and in the galley. It was one hell of a mess. Two bunks broke loose from their moorings.

We survived the first shot, then over the loudspeaker came the words of the captain: "Stow that gun and do not fire again." Then he said he would rather die from an enemy torpedo than from our own firing.

After securing the gun and cleaning up from our disastrous firing, we were all assigned different positions on the other guns. They included six 20mm guns – two forward and two aft and two on the bridge – and a 3"/50 on the bow. I was assigned to one on the bridge. For those who may need info on the guns, a 20 millimeter gun is a rapid-fire machine gun mounted on a pedestal, and each magazine contains 250 shells. A 3"/50 fires a self-contained projectile three inches in diameter and about 30 inches long.

C H A P T E R   4

BATTLE STATIONS

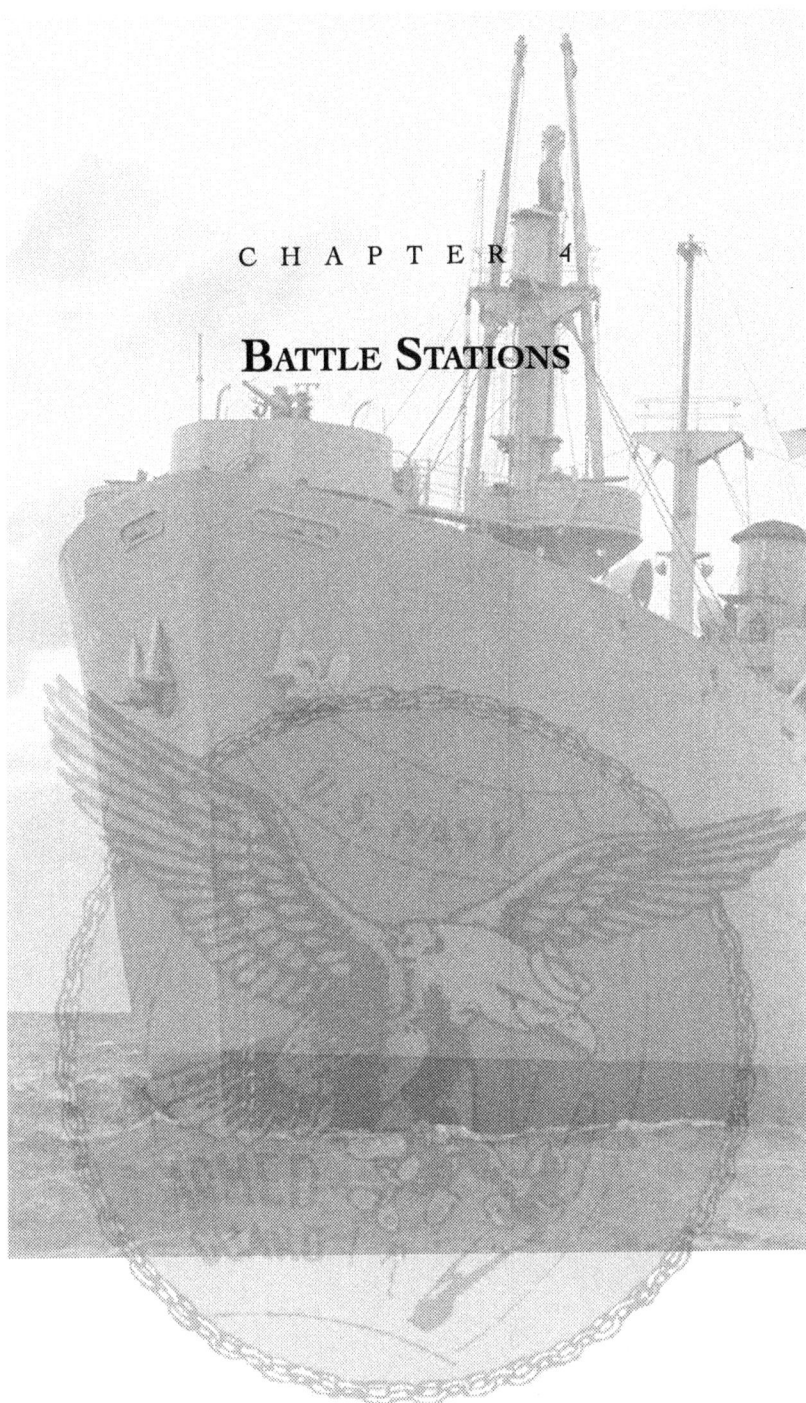

CHAPTER 4

After seven days of sailing in coffin corner, an armed guard member sounded the alarm for all men to report to battle stations. I was on watch at the time on the bridge. When the guns are not used, they are covered by a large canvas bag. I also had earphones on that were connected by a cord to the gun deck. When the alarm sounded, I tried to remove the canvas while in a stage of fright from the announcement. I mean I was really scared. I went looking for the rope that secured the canvas. I ran around the gun tub looking (I think three times), forgetting about the earphones. When I realized this, I was practically tied up. What was an alarm turned out to be a shiny object in the water that the sailor thought was the light of a periscope. About that time the first mate came out of the bridge and saw me tied up and started to laugh, then helped me get unwound. I never did get the canvas off. That was my first encounter with a battle station alarm. Thank God it was false. I soon got over my fear. At other times there were real alarms.

We continued on. I guess the Germans, if they saw our ship, thought it would sink by itself, so why bother to waste a torpedo. There were three ships lost in our convoy, we found out later from our radio operator. We were then glad we were in coffin corner and not in the main convoy.

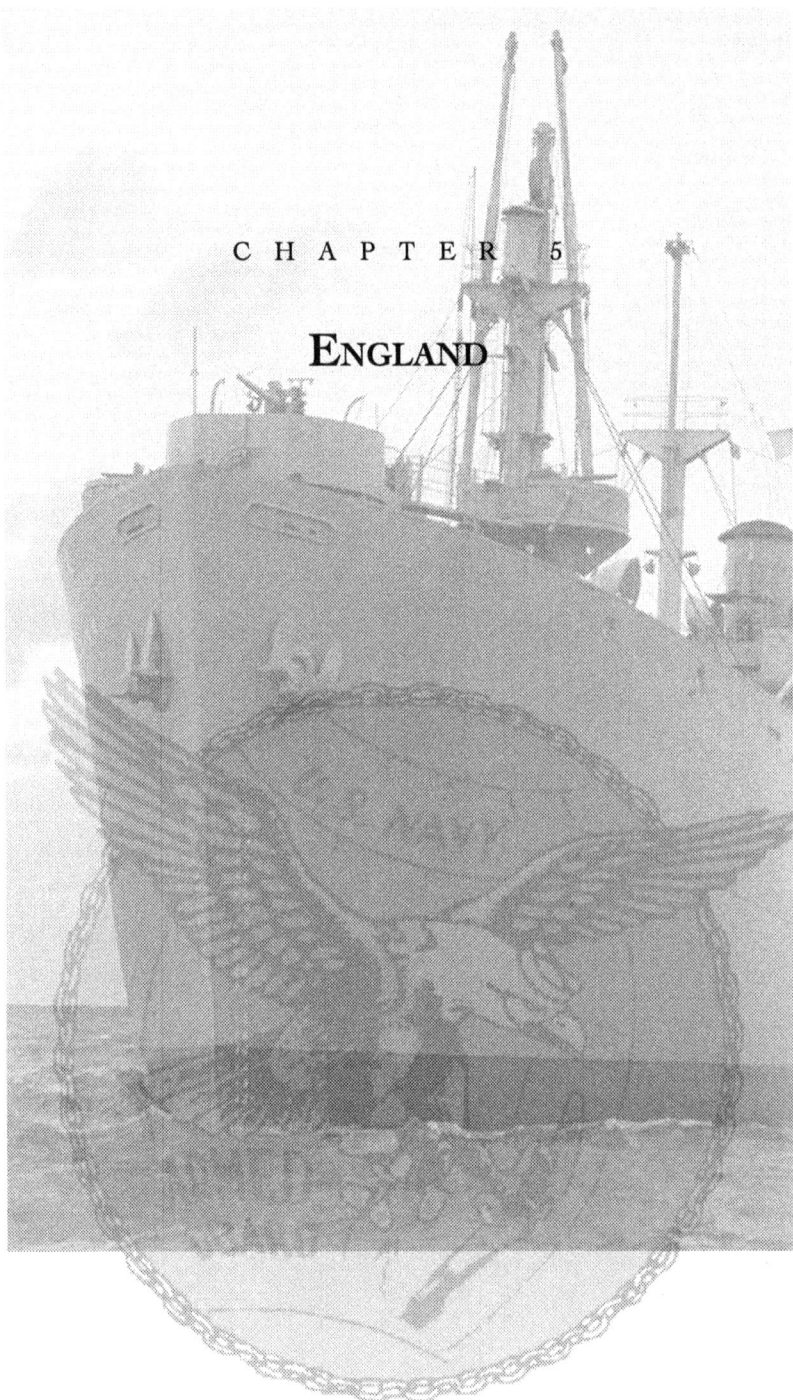

CHAPTER 5

ENGLAND

CHAPTER 5

After what seemed an eternity we were arriving in England. We were heading up the main channel of the Thames River on our way to London. We were put forward of the other ships headed for different locations because the unloading docks for tankers were the last ones up the river. We had no barrage balloons because we were first.

We were all standing at our battle stations, which is normal procedure when entering a harbor, when out of the blue we saw a JU88 bomber and others about to bomb us. Someone yelled, "Hit the deck!" We all dropped like hot potatoes, and on our way down the gun went off and there was a great explosion in front of us. We had just hit the lead bomber dead on. The other bombers peeled off in another direction. We did not know why the gun went off until the man with the gun's firing lanyard told us: he said the lanyard caught in the sleeve of his jacket, and on the way down the gun fired when he went to hit the deck. We were all considered heroes when we met the other seamen at the Queen Arms Pub in London. None of the armed guard told the other seamen how it happened; we just asked them, "What did you think of that shot?"

After we had had a few drinks in the Queen's Pub, a sailor from another ship came running in and said that the limeys were beating up on us American sailors across in the King's Pub. This was the fastest knockout I can remember in history. All the people, including me, ran over to help. I reached the door of the pub and something hit me, and when I woke up it was all over. I had a terrible headache and a scrape on my face that looked like a hobnailed boot mark. After that we returned to the ship. When we unloaded our cargo, we loaded up with a ballast of water and got underway back to the U.S.

C H A P T E R   6

RETURN VOYAGE: HURRICANE

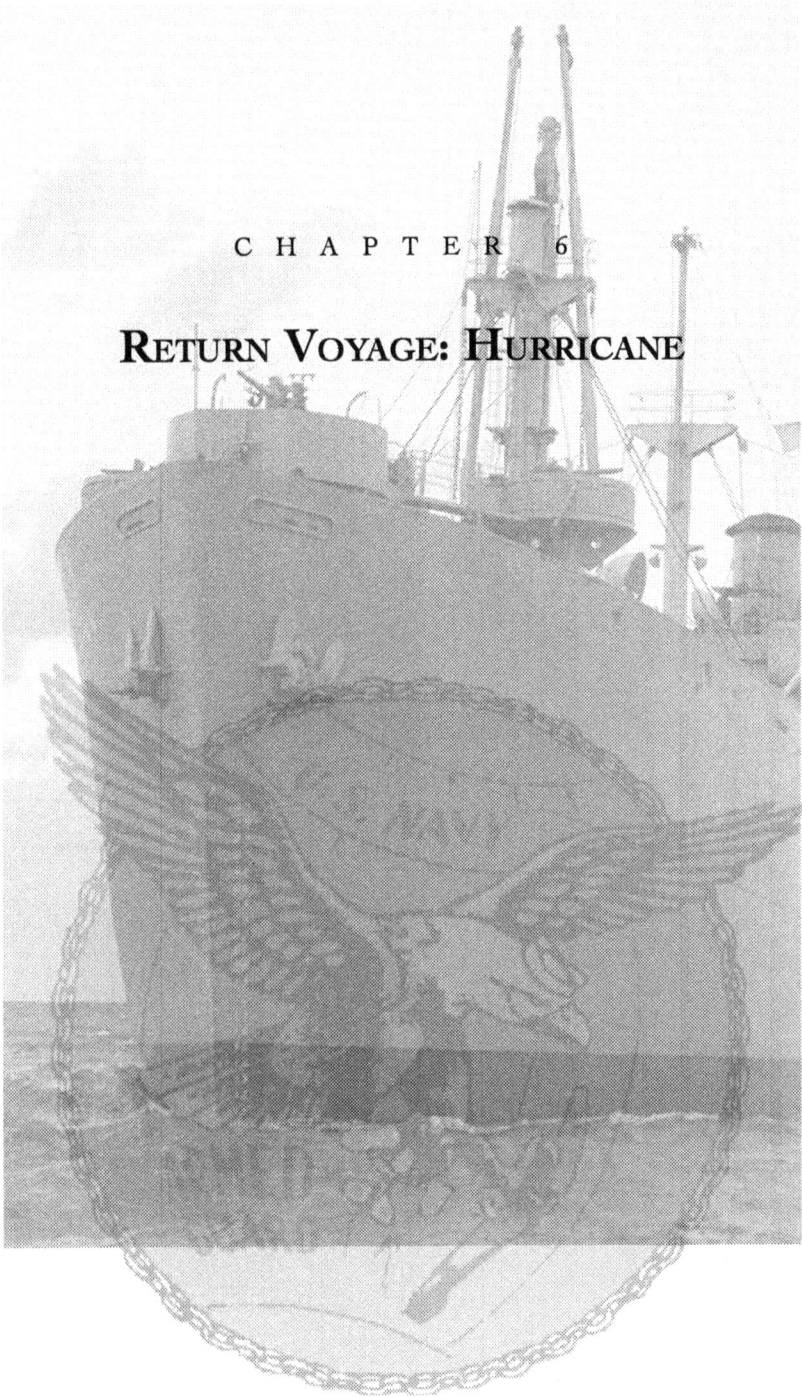

CHAPTER 6

After only 48 hours we were out to sea in a new convoy. After two days at sea we were in the beginning of a horrible hurricane. All the seamen that were amidships and those aft were told to stay put. We were to use the catwalk for chow only. I never knew how bad a hurricane could be. I definitely had no worries about getting sunk. Our captain said we could stand a 50-degree roll, but no more. We hit 48 degrees and then righted ourselves. That was very scary. I stayed on the bridge and watched the seas break over the bow and hit the portholes. It looked as if five fire hoses were blasting the portholes at the same time.

Sometimes the bow was under water. We finally hit the center of the hurricane, even though we were going ahead ten miles and backward four miles every day. On our starboard rear aft there was a ship converted to be an aircraft carrier. I think it was called *CVE*; it was a British ship. Two biplanes took off in the center of the hurricane when it was calm. They were gone approximately 15 minutes when all hell broke loose again. We stood on the fantail and watched the pilots try to land. One hit the deck and exploded. The other was approaching the carrier when the carrier went up and the pilot went under the bow. Both pilots were lost.

We could never understand why they were sent aloft in the first place.

During the hurricane I thought I was getting seasick. The chief mate gave me pickled onions, and I felt a lot better. I don't recommend this, but it worked on me.

We rode the hurricane all the way to New York. It took us 30 days to go from England to the U.S. We ended up with a crack amidships and one in the engine room. We were taken directly to dry dock in Bayonne, New Jersey.

CHAPTER 7

SOUTH AMERICA

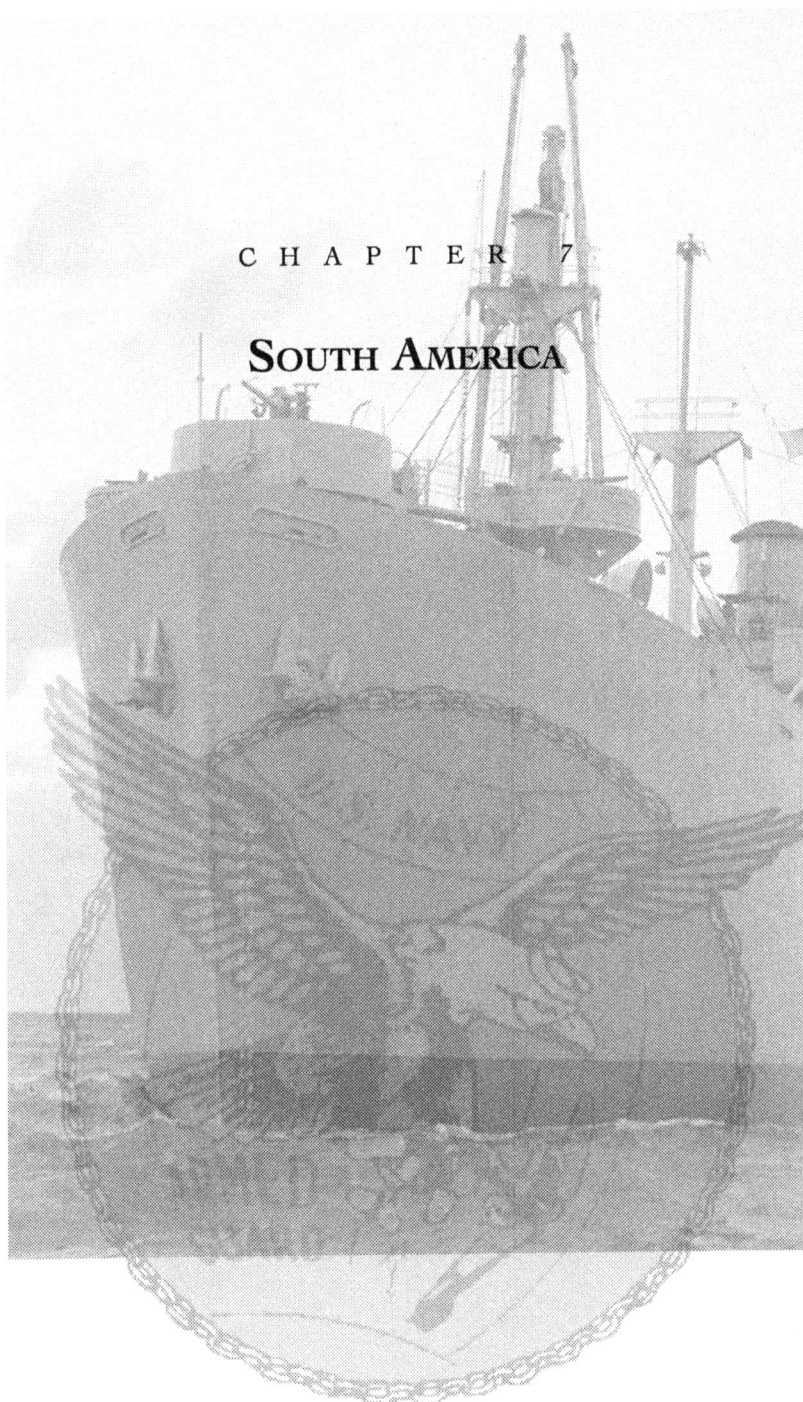

CHAPTER 7

The same chief told me the ship would not be fit for Atlantic duty any more, so see if I could request to stay aboard. I did and started my new adventure in the armed guard.

This was a really good decision. We were scheduled to go to South America, and we did. I was the only armed guard seaman to request to stay. With a new gun crew and gunnery officer we were again under way. They never did replace the 5"/51. We carried it along as a keepsake.

We first went to Aruba and had liberty. We picked up bunker oil and took it to Uruguay to be refined into fuel oil. While there, we went sightseeing in Montevideo. We even went to a picnic put on by the Hormel Meatpacking Company. We left and delivered our cargo to Rio de Janeiro. We had two days of sightseeing: Sugarloaf Mountain and Corkavado. We saw the statue of Christ on top of the mountain. This was like a cruise paid for by the U.S. Navy.

We then picked up gas and delivered it back to Aruba. What a pleasure cruise! We had fresh fruit and real orange juice, fresh eggs, and anything we wanted to eat. We then left Aruba and went to Venezuela, up what they called the Caripito River. It was like going back in time. We were at sea about three days and on the river two days. Don't quote me, but it wasn't a very long trip. When we arrived at our destination it was only a pipeline out of the jungle and into the river. We were allowed to go ashore to the only building there, a bar for the employees and guests. It took only 48 hours to load more bunker oil. This time the captain said we could take three torpedoes and still stay afloat.

On the second day a few of us went back to the bar. We left after a few beers and returned to the ship. There were signs in English that read "Stay on catwalk only." We were only about 50 feet from the jungle. We had a gangway from the ship to the shore. There was also a sign saying "No swimming," with pictures of fish on it. A merchant seaman and one gun-crew member ignored these signs when they jumped into the river to sober up. They found out right away what the signs meant when the piranhas came at them. Fortunately, they got out in time. They sobered up quickly.

After that experience we got loaded and proceeded to return to Aruba. Boy, what duty! After discharging our cargo we were then loaded with some kind of oil and made the same trip back to Rio. We were only ten miles out at sea and even ran with some of our running lights on. We could see the outline of all the cities. Again, more sightseeing in Rio. This time we even went to the horse races for two days. Some war! This trip would have cost over twenty thousand dollars in today's money, and I got it all for free. After Rio we returned to Montevideo, Uruguay. You guessed it: more sightseeing. We even got to see the *Graf Spey*, a German battle ship scuttled in the harbor when the British Navy was waiting for it to come out, even before the U.S. got into the war. While on shore, we had a large steak and tomatoes for lunch, almost as good as the food we were getting aboard the good old *Esso Dover*. Can you imagine – sometimes we even ran out of fresh milk and fresh orange juice and fresh eggs for breakfast. Really rough duty. Sometimes.

After the war, whenever I told this part of my story to my co-workers at the telephone company, they would kid me and say I was never in the war, only on a pleasure cruise. So far they were right.

In Montevideo we were told this would be the last trip to South America, and we were going to the U.S. after first stopping at Rio one last time. What a heart breaker! In the meantime, we ran into a man selling black leather jackets and cowgirl outfits. We bought them from him and told him we had the money on the ship. He gave us the jackets, and I bought the cowgirl outfits and also a suitcase to carry them home with. The only catch was that we had everything we had bought, and the ship was leaving, so we could not go ashore to pay the man. He stood there shaking his fist at us as we were leaving.

I will come back to this story in a moment.

The signalman on our ship – who never drank, never smoked, was never with a woman – was coaxed ashore by a merchant seaman. When we returned he was feeling no pain. While coming up the gangway, he was laughing and trying to tell us what he had done ashore. He had a suitcase in his hand, which contained three-star Hennessy cognac. The bottom of his suitcase gave way, and out came the bottles. He and another merchant seaman were trying to get some of the bottles that were not broken. Considering the shape they were in, this scene would have been a winner today on "America's Funniest Home Videos." The suitcase was made of cardboard and could not hold the weight. This was the end of my honeymoon cruise.

We returned to Bayonne, New Jersey, and delivered our cargo. No one was sure if the *Esso Dover* was going to sail again, so I was sent back to the Armed Guard Center in Brooklyn. I was given a seven-day leave, and saw all my family and two nieces.

I mention my nieces because they are why I bought the cowgirl outfits. On the return home from South America we got an awful smell coming from our quarters. It was from my suitcase, and when we opened it we found that the cowgirl outfits had not been made of tanned leather. I threw them over the side, along with the leather jacket and the suitcase. So we did not get any bargain after all.

We did help a member of the gun crew smuggle ashore a bunch of watches. He had bought the watches for his father, who was a jeweler. We each wore one off the ship when we went ashore.

CHAPTER 8

THE SS *MARGARET BRENT*

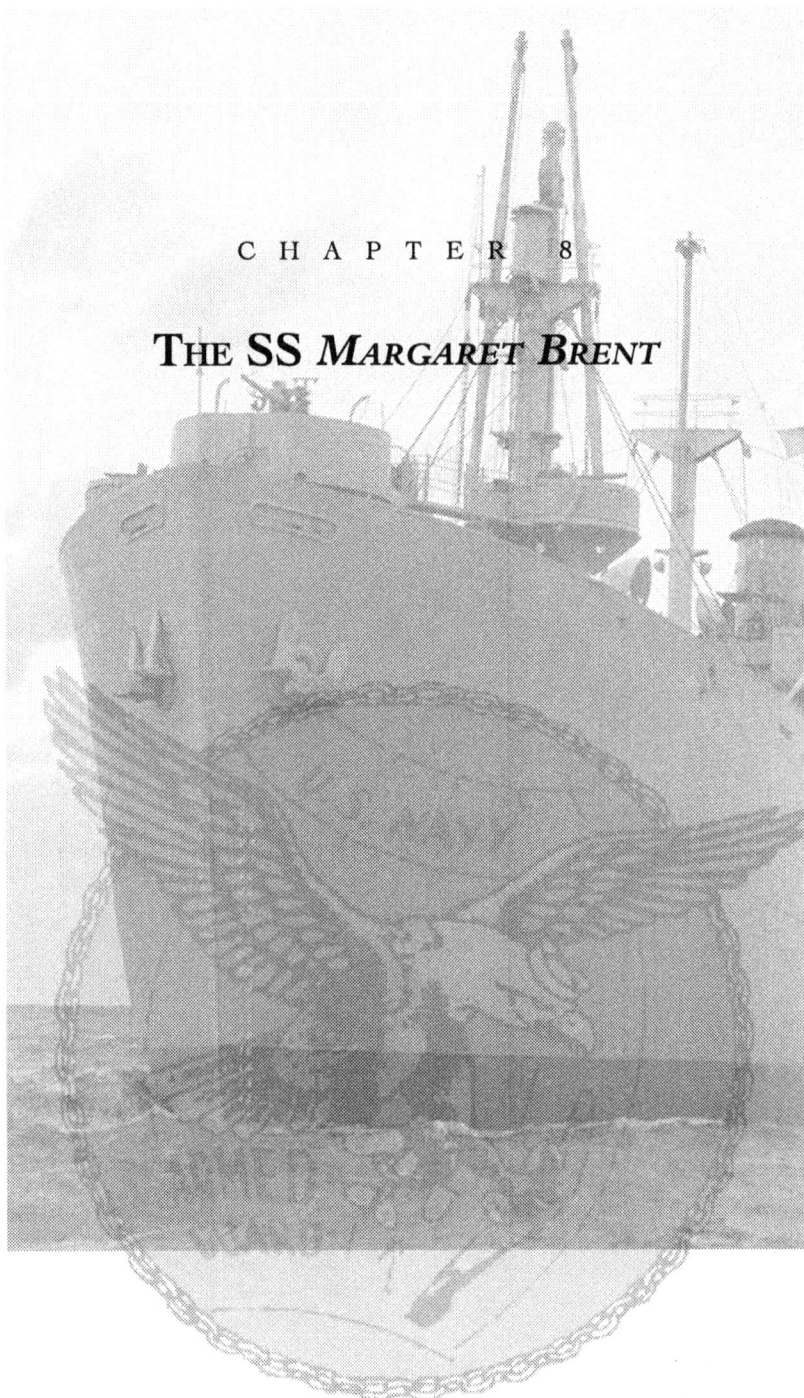

It was now 1944 and I was assigned to the SS *Margaret Brent*. I was now a seaman 1/C. I was again assigned to the bridge. My battle station was a 20 mm gun. Nothing eventful happened on the entire trip; there were no ships lost in the convoy. The ship was a fairly new liberty. We had the same good food that we had on the *Esso Dover*. I was aboard until January 2, 1945.

While aboard the *Margaret Brent*, I passed the tests and became a gunner's mate 3/C. Overall, I thought it was an uneventful trip. We were in on the invasion of Europe on June 6, 1944. We couldn't see what was going on because we were so far out, loaded with 90 mm ammunition. After four days we were allowed to come in and get unloaded. They unloaded us in record time, and we were on our way back to the U.S.A.

THE SS *WILLIAM B. ALLISON*

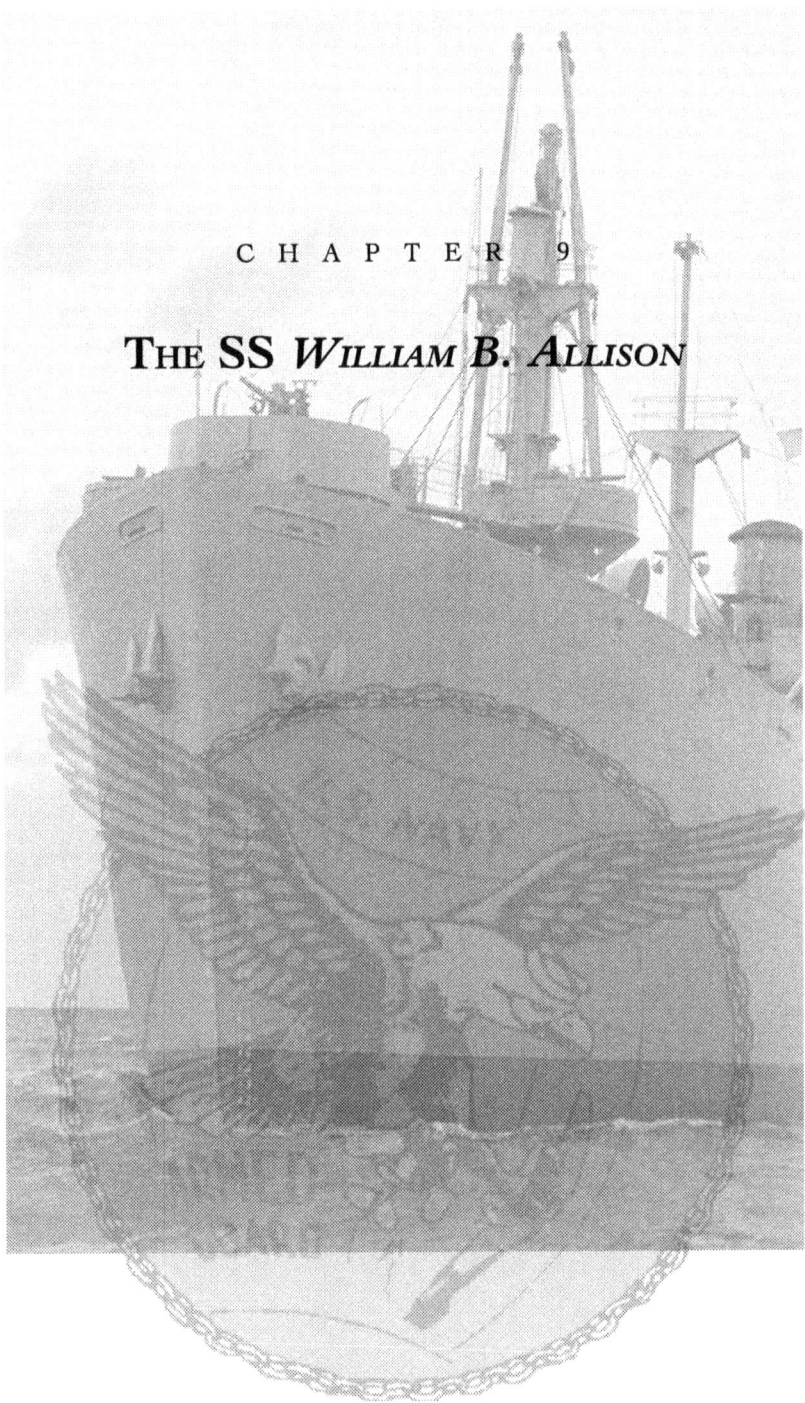

After another leave home I was assigned to the fateful *William B. Allison*, or *Willie B.*, as we called it. We then went to the South Pacific, the Russell Islands, but not in convoy. There we picked up a seabee battalion, and our next stop was Eniwetok.

Editor's note: Henry Valli's account of this voyage adds the following general information about the William B. Allison and its crew:

On January 24, 1945, I reported aboard the SS *William B. Allison* as a gunner's mate second class. Our gunnery officer was Bernard O'Connell, lieutenant junior grade. Also aboard were gunner's mate third class John Stockton and gunner's mate third class Joseph Ninteman. Some of the other Armed Guard crew members were John Belluss, seaman 1/c; Delmar Lafferty, seaman 1/c; P. V. Harris, seaman 1/c; Ernest Metcalf, seaman 1/c; L. Jones, seaman 1/c; G. J. Hermin, seaman 1/c; and W. C. Strain, seaman 1/c. We had a signalman but I've forgotten his name.

The ship was armed with a 3"/50 in the bow, eight 20 mm's (4 on each side of the ship), and a 5"/ 38 aft. There were also smoke canisters on the aft of the ship. We did not have a full compliment of gunners (28). We had a skeleton crew because we were not scheduled to go into a battle zone.

My assignment called for the overall responsibility of the guns and assigning the men on watch. I had control of the 5"/38 aft. Joe Ninteman had the 3"/50 forward, and John Stockton had the eight 20 mm's. All of the navy crew had experience aboard other ships except Harris, who was 17 years old and had never been aboard a ship. I believe that this was Lt. Jg O'Connell's first trip. I think that he was a school teacher in civilian life. The lieutenant's quarters were midship, and the rest of the navy crew were housed in the aft of the ship.

CHAPTER 10

LEAVING NEW YORK

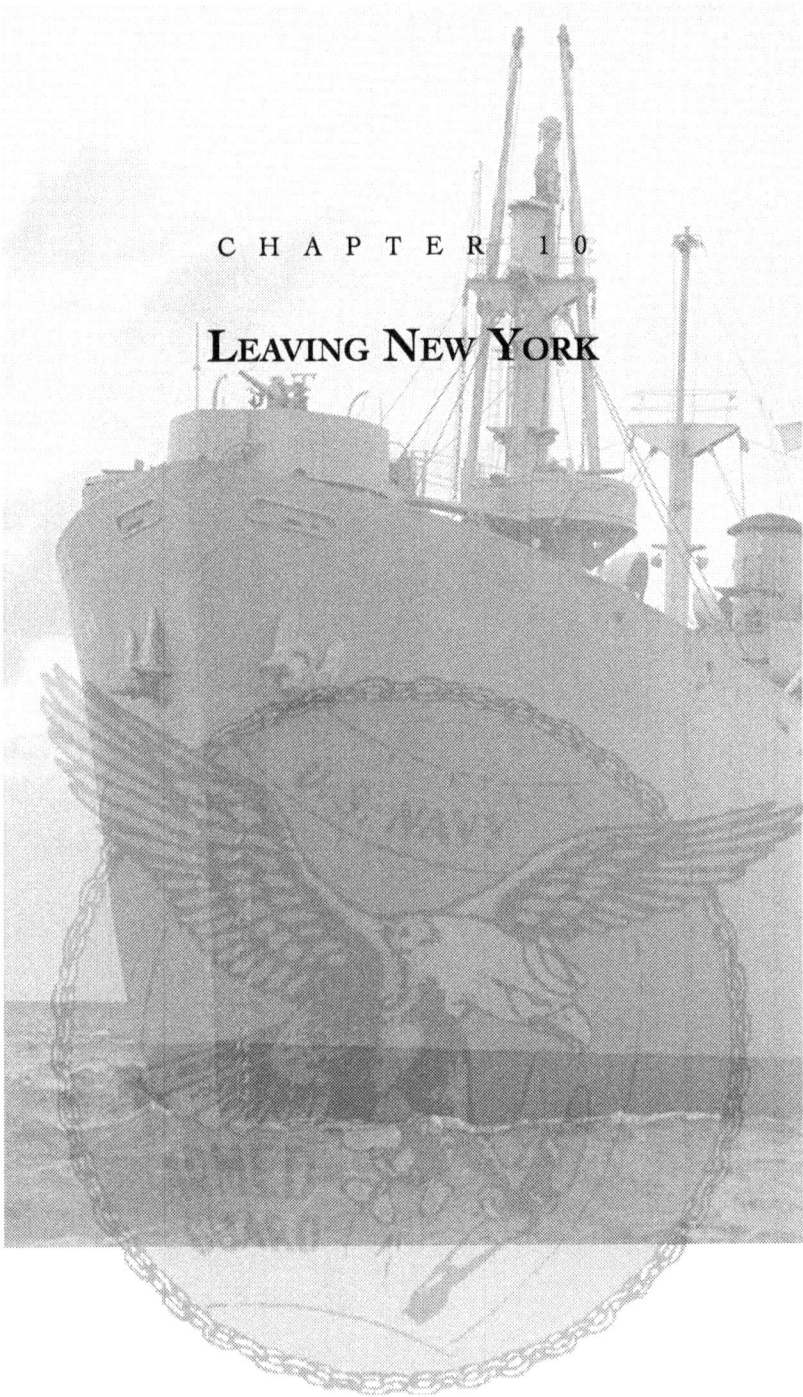

CHAPTER 10

Editor's note: This chapter was written by Asa Casterlin, a merchant marine who served as the ship's second radio operator on this voyage of the Allison.

On February 20, 1945, final operations were being made for sailing. The booms were rigged down for sea and all was in readiness, but no sailing orders came until late in the day to take effect the next morning. That afternoon and throughout the night, a wet snow fell and froze, making the ship a mass of ice about an inch thick.

Finally, on the 21st at about 8 a.m. we let go the bow lines and stern lines, and with the aid of two tugboats shoved out into the stream, New York's upper bay. We had a Mackay radio technician on board who calibrated the radio direction finder with a station on Governors Island. That was accomplished by noon. Then we set out for sea, dropping the pilot and the Mackay man when out of the harbor.

About two days out of New York and somewhere off Cape Hatteras, the snow melted and the weather became warm enough to sit on deck without a shirt on. At the same time the sea became rough, and almost everyone on board went around with a haggard look that marks the transition between land legs and sea legs. The Atlantic Ocean was beautiful, however, and I saw my first flying fish gliding from wave to wave. The sea was a sea of continuous white-caps and the swells were coming at us from ahead. The ship would rear up, stop momentarily, then plunge into the next wave.

As we approached the Bahama Islands it calmed down somewhat. The weather, by this time, was very warm and pleasant. We steered through Crooked Island Passage, then through Windward Passage, where we caught a good look at Cape Maise, Cuba. The next two days were taken up in spanning the Caribbean Sea.

C H A P T E R   1 1

LIFE ABOARD SHIP

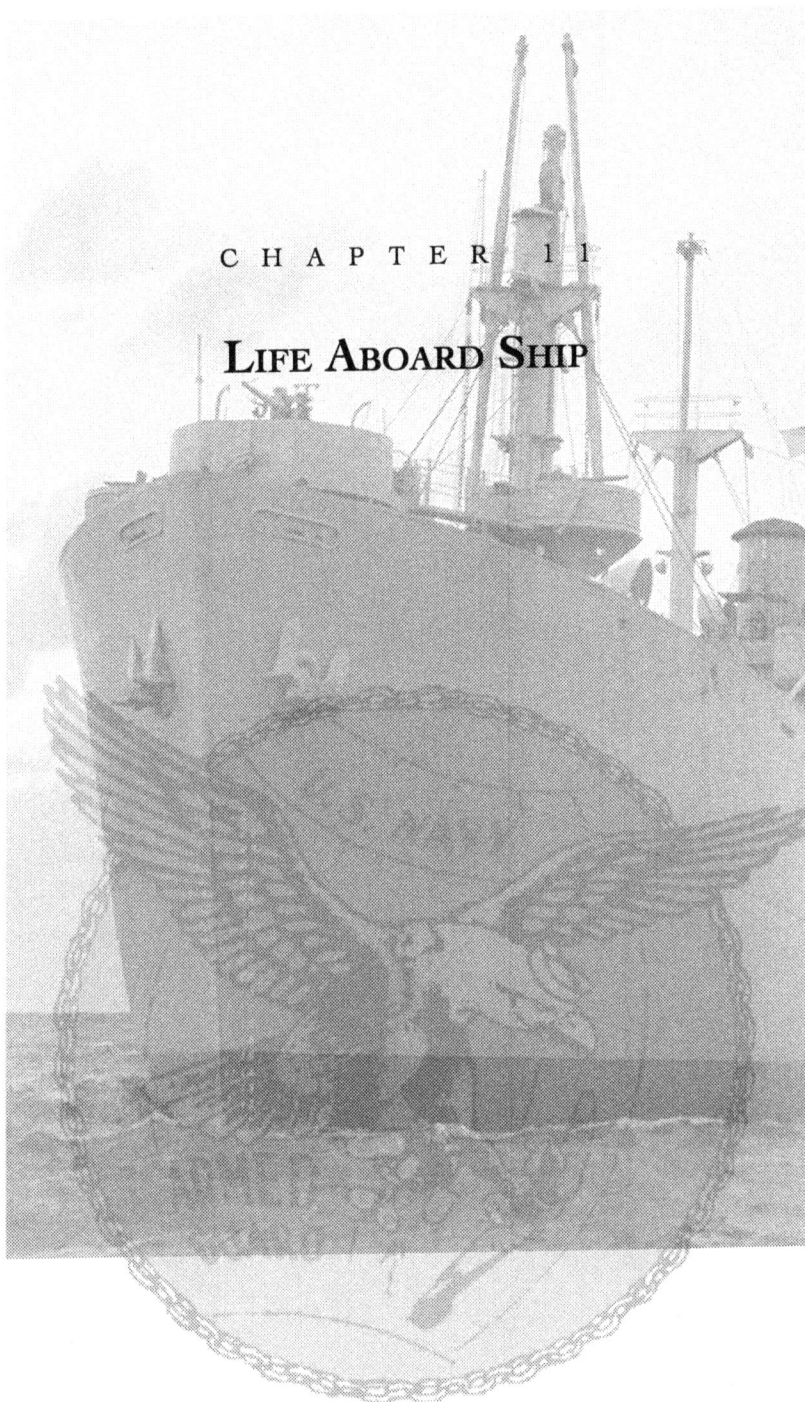

CHAPTER 11

Editor's note: This chapter was written by armed guard member Henry Valli, who was John Stockton's cabin mate on this voyage of the Allison.

Our mess hall was separate from the merchant crew. The naval personnel stuck together mostly and had minimum contact with the merchant crew. We cleaned the guns to keep them from rusting, and stood watches 24 hours a day. The lieutenant would not let us test fire the guns, so training was going through the motions of loading and firing, and studying the maintenance of the guns from manuals.

There is no recreation aboard a merchant vessel, so the crew played cards, rolled dice, read, smoked cigarettes, and fought one another. When you hear a story for the tenth time, tempers flare. While we might have fought among ourselves, there was still a comradeship, and if someone else caused a dispute he had to contend with the whole crew.

John Stockton and I shared a cabin under the 5"/38. The room was on the port side and was about 5 feet wide by 10 feet long. It had two bunks, one above the other, and two lockers side by side, each being about 15 inches wide and 12 inches deep and 6 feet high. We also had a porthole in the cabin. We only slept in the quarters since there was no room to sit down. We could only sleep or read in our bunks.

The crew would stand watch for four hours and have eight hours off. When you were not on duty, you worked on the guns, chipped paint, did your laundry, wrote letters, or did other chores.

Being aboard a ship is an experience you will never forget. When the sea is calm and you are underway during the day, you can see the porpoises and the flying fish leaping out of the water leading your ship, a wisp of smoke on the horizon, or a distant traveler. The sky is a deep blue with billowing white clouds. The sea is blue green near the ship and gets darker the further you look toward the horizon until the sea looks black. The air's slight breeze is crisp and clean and smells of salt, and as you breathe deeply it leaves you feeling elated. Terns and pelicans scream in excitement as they search the sea for their next morsel. The gentle rolling of the ship lulls you into a feeling of contentment.

Toward the evening, as the sun goes down it is a large orange ball that settles into the sea. All the colors around you continually change. Finally, the stars start to appear, and as the sky gets darker a million stars light up the ship so you don't need a light to walk around the ship. The moon appears, adding to the magnificence of the heavens.

During the night the ship's tubes blow out the accumulated

soot through the ship's stack. If you left your laundry out, it would be covered with soot. In the small hours of the morning, as you leave your watch to get a cup of coffee, you can smell the bread that is being baked in the coal-fired stoves. As the night wanes, the stars start to disappear, and the horizon starts to get lighter until the sun starts to come up out of the sea. The colors all around you change again, and a new day is at hand.

When the wind comes up, the seas become choppy, slapping against the side of the ship. The sea starts to swell and the bow of the ship plunges into the rolling waves, sending a fine spray over the bow. The spray strikes your face and wets the deck. The wind blows the water off your face and off the deck. After a short time you can feel the salt that has been deposited on your face, and when you lick your lips you can taste the salt. Your eyes burn and it becomes harder to blink.

If a gale develops, the deck becomes awash with the sea. Lifelines will have to be strung so that you will not be washed overboard. It becomes impossible to stay in your bunk. You must hold on to something, and you will wait for your chow until the blow subsides. Again, all the colors change around you. The clouds are black and heavy, and sometimes the ship plows through the clouds that are low. The ship rolls, pitches, and shudders as it goes from one swell into another. In one minute the bow is under water and the fantail is out of the water, with the screw flailing at the air. When the fantail strikes the water, the entire ship shudders. The metal of the ship creaks and groans from the strain, and you hope to God it doesn't break up.

Each day the sea brings something different, sometimes a squall that lasts 10 to 15 minutes to thoroughly drench you, only to leave you hot and sweltering from the humidity. In the same day the air can become dry and the deck of the ship unbearably hot, or it can become a combination of all the conditions that can arise.

CHAPTER 12

FISHING IN THE CARIBBEAN

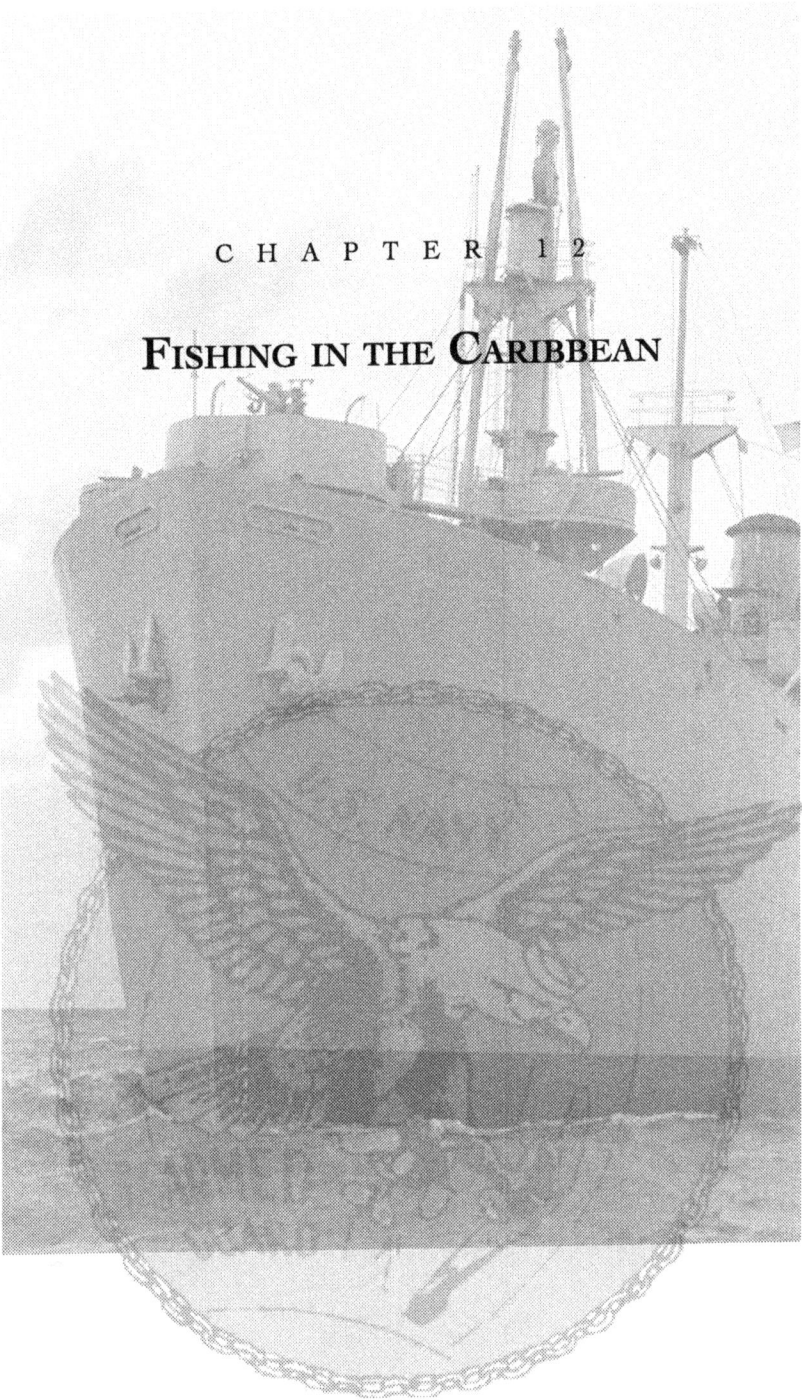

I remember when a few of the gun crew, with the help of the merchant men, made a fishing pole. Our first attempt was getting a piece of pipe from the chief engineer, who also made our hook by using a piece of steel rod, bending it and welding on a barb, then placing a white rag over the hook. We placed the pipe on the railing, and they welded a clamp onto the railing to hold it in place. Then we attached clothesline to it and started to fish. Our first attempt was a disaster. We never thought we would catch anything, but we did. The fish bent the pole because we did not have anything to take the strain. So it was back to the drawing board. This time we took the springs out of our bunks and placed them on the railing and then attached them to the pole. This let the pole move as if we were playing the fish. After that we caught a large kingfish. We could not reel it in, so we asked for steam on deck. This worked fine, and we put the rope on the capstan and reeled it in. We gave it to the cook, who filleted it and cooked it up for all the crew. It weighed about 80 pounds.

Editor's note: Henry Valli wrote the following account of fishing with this bed-spring rig:

One day when underway in the Caribbean, the boys threw a log line overboard with a meat hook attached with rotten meat on it. They rigged the line so that it was coiled on the deck, with a bed-spring coil attached to the line and to the chain on the railing. When a fish took the hook it stretched the spring, and while the line was paying out, one of the crew grabbed the line to stop it. It only took a moment for the line to burn both of his hands. When the fish stopped running they hauled it in, hitting the shark with a baseball bat. The shark was about five and a half feet long. The merchant marines' cook skinned the shark, taking the meat along both sides of the backbone, and baked it with tomatoes and spices. It was very good.

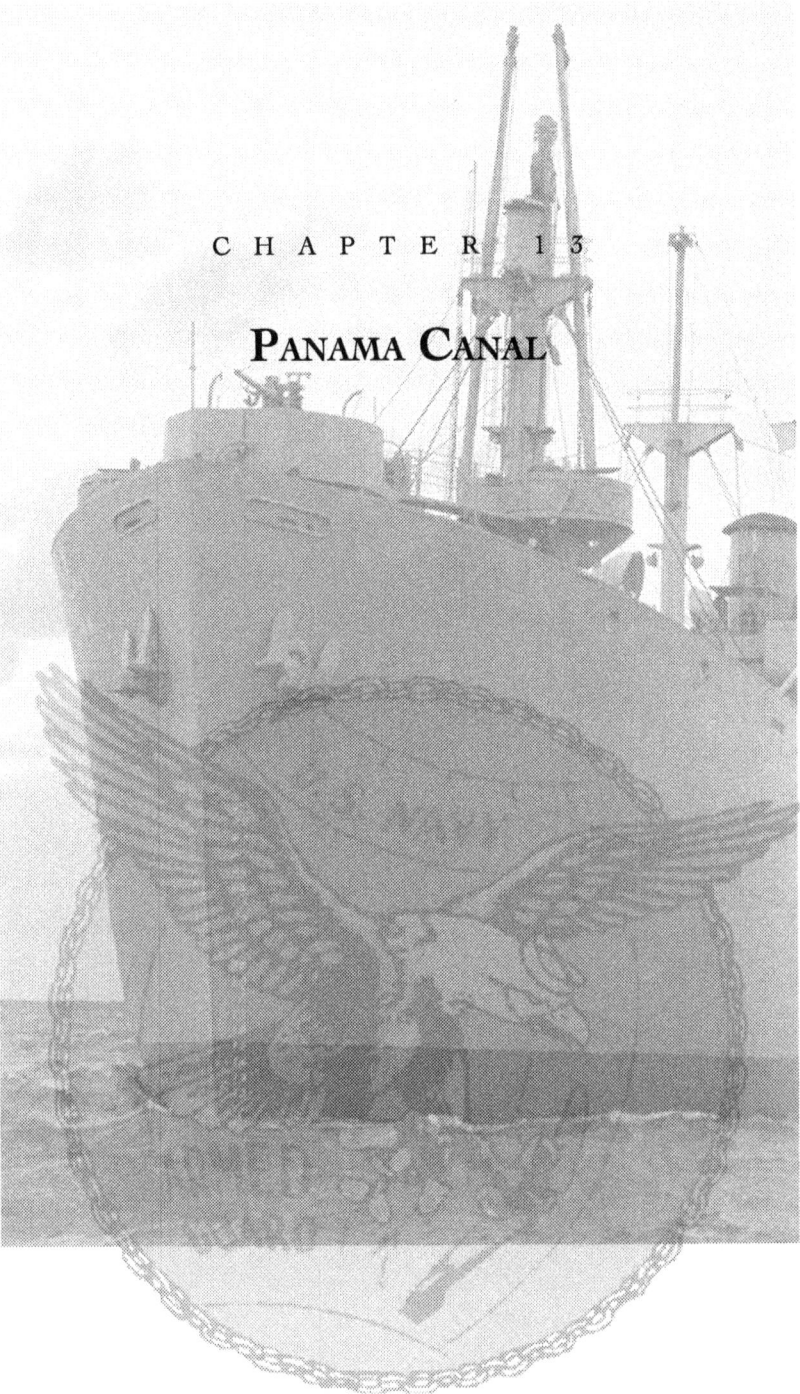

CHAPTER 13

PANAMA CANAL

Editor's note: This chapter, which describes the ship's passage through the Panama Canal around March 1, 1945, was written by Asa Casterlin.

We then came upon the Panama Canal, just eight days after leaving New York. To say it is well protected and patrolled would be an understatement. Planes are continually in the air overhead, the entire zone bristles with anti-aircraft guns and coast-defense guns, all well concealed, and patrol craft are constantly on watch at both ends. We were picked up about three miles out by a pilot, and as we passed the nets we were boarded by three separate boarding parties. The first was a nervous Spaniard who thought himself very important. He represented the steamship company in Panama, brought our mail aboard, and arranged for washing our linen and sending it to the other end of the canal via railroad so we might have it before leaving. A navy boarding party came on and sealed up the transmitters so they could not be used going through the canal. A couple of these navy men stayed aboard to use our receiver in going through the canal. A third boarding party consisted of about 15 marines armed with carbines. They immediately scattered and went to sleep with their carbines stacked in a corner, a state in which they stayed throughout the canal journey.

We lay at anchor at the Atlantic entrance of the canal, just off the beautiful city of Cristobal, until about 10 a.m., then proceeded through the canal, with a canal official, of course, in complete charge of running the ship. The first set of locks, and the largest, were the Gatun Locks, which lifted us up into Gatun Lake. The ship went into the lock under its own power, but was then hooked onto mechanical "mules" which ran on cog-wheel tracks along either side of the lock. These mules, which were made by the General Electric Company, were attached to the ship by large steel cables and traveled at one speed on the level and up the grade between locks. This grade was surprisingly steep for any locomotive, being, it appeared, at least a 60-degree angle from the horizontal.

Gatun Lake is a beautiful body of fresh water dotted with numerous small islands. There was much activity on the lake, with almost every type of craft anchored there, even submarines. There was also what appeared to be an exclusive yacht club with numerous sailboats going through the lake at about three knots. We took advantage of the fresh water and washed down the decks with our fire hose system. At the opposite end of Gatun Lake, we were lowered through another set of locks to a long dug portion of the canal. Dense vegetation lined the banks, including an occasional coconut palm. It was then quite evident what a huge undertaking the Panama Canal was. Just at nightfall we were lowered through another set of locks into the bay at the Pacific side, where we went into a navy dock and took on oil and water and some supplies.

Across the bay was Balboa, C.Z., and its adjacent Panama City, where we went that evening for shore leave. A naval launch took us across the bay with great formality, the officers sitting in the dry part of the launch and entering and leaving first. At Balboa a fleet of taxis were waiting to get us over into Panama City, a city which is well prepared and eager to separate Americans from their money. At Balboa, navy officials checked the amount of money we had with us and the amount we brought back.

A taxi driver herded us into his broken down 1940 job, and after the second mate dickered with him for ten minutes in Spanish, he agreed to take us to Panama City for 75 cents each. In that car he would have made money if he had taken us for 10 cents each. On the way he tried to sidetrack us to get us to hire his cab for a trip to the "Villa Amor," which is a government-supervised (it is said) house of prostitution some six miles up in the Panamanian mountains. We, however, being all clean-living gents, went into the heart of Panama City and shopped at the souvenir stores which lined the streets. Also lining the streets were hordes of automobiles, all nationalities, all ages, all makes, and all yelling the same thing, "V. Amor!"

After shopping, we stopped in for a milkshake and were surprised to see that all manner of candy, gum, and things unobtainable in the states were very plentiful in Panama. I guess we must keep up the foreign market at the expense of our own citizens. We then went from café to café, which had suddenly sprung up between each souvenir shop, looking for a couple of our officers that had strayed. We drank in only one café, where we had a bottle of Panamanian brew. In the others we were too busy beating off the designing women, mostly pretty-beaten-up old bags, but occasionally we saw a nice-looking one, probably 16 years old and new at the game. We escaped unscathed and returned to the ship via the 12 o'clock boat.

The next day we were confined to the naval depot where we were anchored, but there we had a PX and got a haircut and stored up on candy and gum and cigars.

CHAPTER 14

CROSSING THE PACIFIC

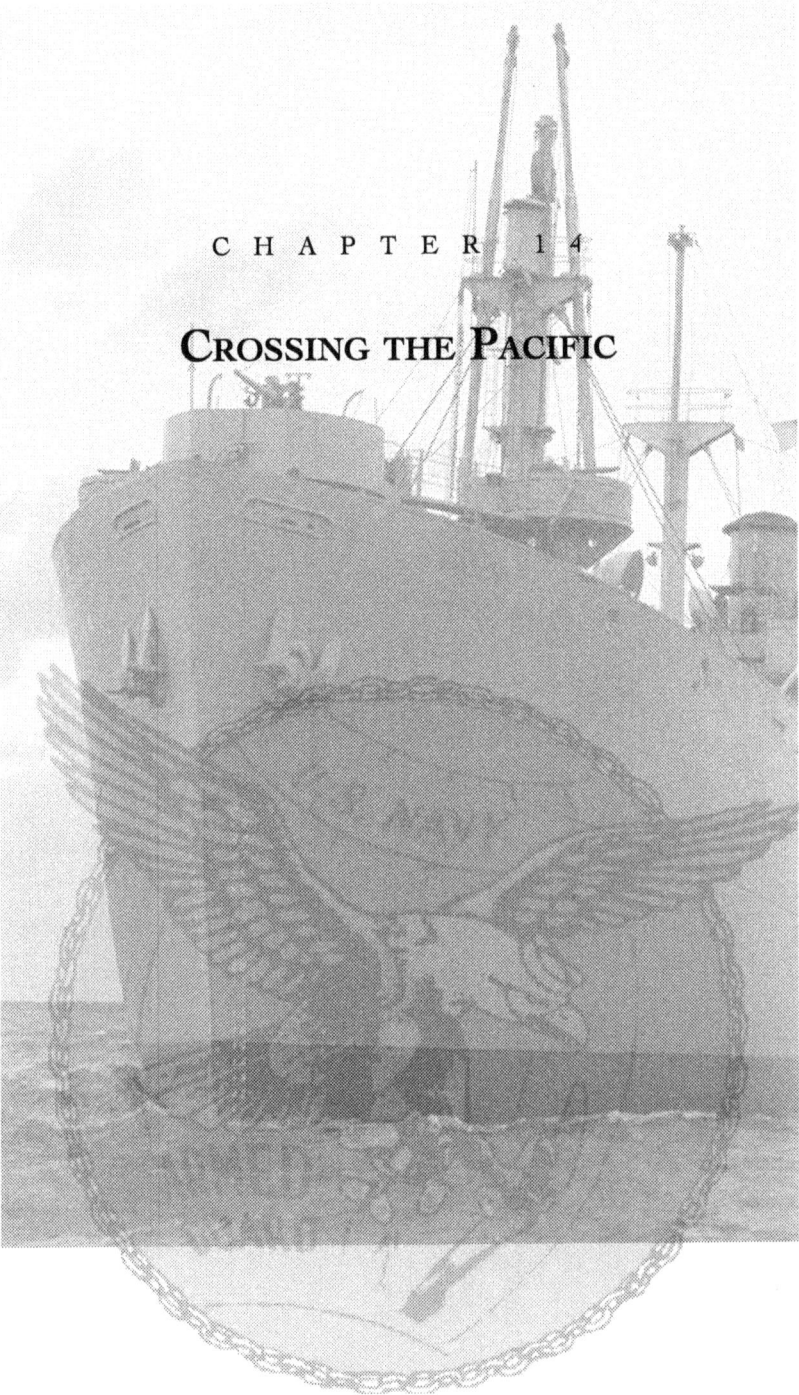

CHAPTER 14

Editor's note: This chapter, written by Asa Casterlin, describes the ship's long crossing of the Pacific in March of 1945.

We put out into the blue Pacific for the next leg of our voyage on March 3, 1945. One can imagine how long and drawn out a Pacific crossing can be in a liberty ship by imagining oneself riding across the continent of America and back at 13 miles per hour without stopping. Our Pacific trip took 26 days from leaving Panama until we caught sight of the towering peaks of Espiritu Santo, NLW Hebrides. The length of the journey gave everyone ample chance to become acquainted and to settle down in their respective jobs. Personalities began to show themselves, and private lives came to the front at sundown after supper when everyone off watch would gather on the port side of the boat deck to smoke and "chew the fat." This gathering later became known unofficially as "the port side athletic club." Talking and expectorating were the most strenuous games indulged in, although a contest sprang up between the chief engineer and the purser as to which one could put more cigarette ashes in the other fellow's pocket.

The crossing of the Pacific was marked with exceptionally nice weather, almost invariably a following sea, and usually just breezy enough to keep the ship tolerably cool. A great percentage of the journey was in the immediate vicinity of the equator, and during the day the quarters warmed up considerably. But we could always cool off on deck and be lulled to sleep by a slap in our low-pressure cylinder, which could be heard all over the ship and sounded quite ominous. Whatever ailed it was repaired, however, at Espiritu Santo, by our competent first assistant engineer.

The true beauty of the sea came out in that crossing. At night the sunsets were beautiful beyond description, and in the morning the sunrises rivaled them. The placid Pacific stretched out on every side in a seeming endless expanse of chameleon-like waters, ever changing in color as the cloud formations changed. After the sun had set and complete darkness surrounded the blacked-out ship, hordes of phosphorescent animals and plant life became visible along the wake of the ship and where here and there an occasional white cap was stirred up. This luminescent effect made the ship appear to be plowing through deep snow, while along the sides of the ship larger animals could be seen glowing with an eerie blue light. In the daytime we could always see the flying fish dart out of one wave into another, thinking, perhaps, that the ship was some gigantic thing after them.

The crossing dragged out into 28 days, and long before the 28th day life became more and more a routine. Every 15 degrees of longitude we would move the clocks back an hour, which would change the hours of radio watches. This was the only thing that changed. Mondays would be washday for me, and Sundays would be a rest day when I didn't lift my finger to do anything I didn't have to do. Sundays, Mr. Evans and I would put on a white shirt and comb our hair just a little better just to remind the rest of the crew that is was Sunday. Every other day of the week was just a matter of finding a cool place to sit and whittle, read Sherlock Holmes stories, or just observe the beauties of the southern Pacific. Occasionally we would spot a school of porpoises jumping through the water gracefully.

On the 23rd day we sighted our first land. It looked so good to me. I was all for going and building a house on it and living there for the rest of my life. It turned out to be a small volcanic island, uninhabited, but it looked good to me. From then on to Espiritu Santo we sighted land every day, distant islands of the Ellice and Santa Cruz groups.

Left: John Stockton, Dover, NJ, 1944.
Above: John Stockton and Nick Nito at boot
camp, 1943. Below left: John Stockton home on
leave in Rockaway, NJ.

Alice Williams, circa 1944, the girl John fell in love
with and later married.

Above: John Stockton and Hank Valli, 1990s. Above right: Alice and John Stockton at their home in Spring City, TN, 1990s. Right: Malika, Sylvi, and Ron Stockton at Ron and Sylvi's wedding, 2002. Far right: Patricia Lynne Stockton and Ed Taylor at their wedding, 2001.

Four generations of Stocktons (left to right, top to bottom): Cory Carlson, Taylor Carlson, Ron Stockton, Alice Stockton, John Stockton, Lynne Taylor, Lori Carlson, Brinden Carlson, Ashtyn Carlson.

CHAPTER 15

ESPIRITU SANTO

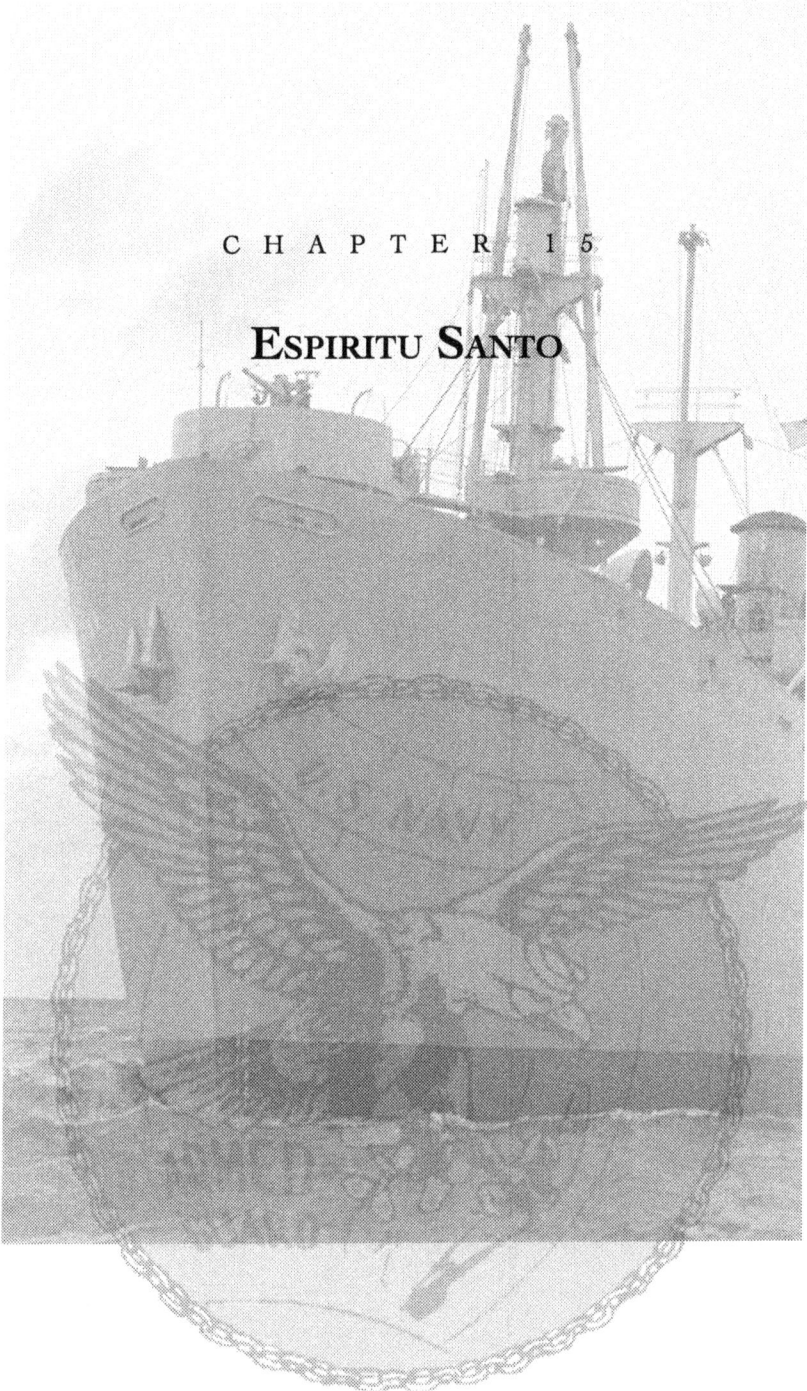

Editor's note: This chapter was written by Asa Casterlin.

Early in the morning of the 28th day, we sighted Espiritu Santo Island, jewel of the New Hebrides group. It is a mountainous volcanic mass of luxuriant vegetation, too hot and buggy for a non-native to live comfortably on, but nonetheless it looked like heaven to us after 28 days of water, water, water.

Espiritu Santo Island is the largest of the New Hebrides. In peace time it was governed by a joint British-French condominium government, which for the New Hebrides, had its main office on Efate Island, also known as Sandwich Island. Santo Island is about 75 miles long and 50 miles wide and is both volcanic and coral in formation. Along the shore the soil is mostly coral sand, but as the elevation increases the soil becomes more volcanic in nature.

As we approached the nets we were met by a pilot who escorted us into Segond Channel, on the southeastern corner, which was lined with docks of a semi-permanent nature and bristling with military activity. In fact, the whole southern rim of the island was one military installation after another, broken up occasionally with a native village or plantation. The army had built a road along the coastline with bulldozers. The packed coral sand made a nice road-bed, but was very dusty when dry and became a mass of mud when wet. This road was constantly alive with jeeps, trucks and every conceivable army motor vehicle. It was evident that there was no gasoline rationing here.

Shortly after we docked, Negro army stevedores came aboard and started unloading our cargo of some 50,000 cases of beer and miscellaneous stores. They worked fast and efficiently, so efficiently in fact that they unloaded our electric toaster from the dining saloon when we weren't looking. They would lift the crates from the hold and set them on the dock; then a small loading machine would come along, pick the crates up, and either put them on a truck or carry them off to a warehouse.

The morning after we docked, we got up early to go ashore. It was quite easy to hitchhike a ride from one end of the island to the other. And it did not take us long to find out just where the various PX's and points of interest were located. Our first excursion was to the army PX about four miles east of our dock # 4. This was the main PX on the island, selling souvenirs, ice cream, popcorn, and the usual clothing and personal items. The souvenirs seemed priced so that someone was profiting well by their sale. Sheepskin rugs from New Zealand were $7.00, carved teakwood bookends from the Fiji's were $6.00, grass skirts from Santo were $3.00, and shell necklaces were various prices. I could not get excited over these souvenirs, especially when I thought of what a similar amount of money would purchase in useful items back in the States. The ice cream-coke-popcorn side of the PX was rather smelly. Hundreds of G.I.'s would gather there in their work clothes, bathed in perspiration. That, combined with the rotting refuse in the refuse cans, made holding one's nose necessary while one was buying and necessitated a quick retreat to neighboring coconut grove with one's ice cream or popcorn. The heat was so intense during midday that the ice cream melted immediately as it came from the freezer.

We immediately marked ourselves as newcomers to the island by picking up fallen coconuts and husking them and eating them. They were quite a novelty, and the old timers would smile knowingly at us and sometimes come up and ask us how things were in the States when we left. They would always mournfully tell us how many months they had been there, which usually was anywhere from 20 to 30. They all agreed it was too long to be stuck on that sizzling isle. When we arrived, summer was just in the process of turning into fall, and the temperature, while still always between 95 and 105 degrees in the daytime, was said to be moderating. As the boys said, "Jeez, it's nothing like it was a month ago!"

While the unloading was going on, we made our little explorations everyday. One day Kawula, Freddie, and I set out for the main native settlement of the island, where the local British-French condominium government office was located. We hitched rides on various vehicles for about six miles and finally got to it. The government building was in the midst of a native settlement and was the only civilized-looking house around. It flew two faded flags, one French and one British. A couple of Melanesians were sitting around in the yard, and on the porch was a very important looking guard, a black boy with a bright red fez on his head, who saluted royally as we approached. The government building was a two-room affair, only one of which seemed to be occupied at the moment. In it was a little fat man completely surrounded by rubber stamps. Never have I seen so many rubber stamps in such a small place; there were racks and racks of them. This little fat man was babbling what sounded like a cross between French and pigeon English to another white man, presumably his secretary. I finally worked up the nerve to interrupt and ask if we could look over the native village.

I asked him, "Do you speak English?"

He said, "No, what do you want?"

This took me back a bit. Undaunted, after a minute I asked my question and he said, "Sure, sure, look it over" and went back to babbling again. So we walked around the native village.

The huts were usually one-room jobs made of miscellaneous boards with thatched roofs. Holes were cut for doors and windows, but they had only curtains to draw over them. Each hut seemed to have its own miniature garden and chicken coop with scrawny chickens running over everything. As we would approach a hut, the native women would draw the curtains so we couldn't look in. When they saw Freddie with his camera, they drew them all the faster. One Tonkinese girl seemed unafraid, and I believe we got her picture. She was about 12 years old and was having the time of her life chasing a poor emaciated chicken around.

The Tonkinese and Melanesians seemed to live together without disturbing one another. The Tonkinese are a mixture, mostly Japanese, and were said to have migrated from Indo-China. They looked Japanese to me, and even had a Shinto Temple in one of the villages. The "natives," or Melanesians, were a friendly black people with curly hair, which they took great delight in bleaching with hydrogen peroxide, when available, or homemade potash. We tried talking with one native, but after plying him with cigarettes we could only get him to say two words: "native" and "Tonkinese." He was pointing out the difference in the kids playing in the yards. We managed a picture of the kids after bribing them with a roll of lifesavers.

Further on into the village was located the local Catholic mission, which consisted of a chapel, hospital, school, and parish house. The hospital was off limits to American troops, but we went up and tried to talk to the sister who was supervising play of her school kids in the yard. The kids were allowed to play with Bowie knives, the ever-present tool/weapon of the Melanesians. A Bowie knife is a sharp knife about 18 inches long, just right for hacking one's way through the jungle, or cutting coconuts off a tree, or just about anything.

The chapel itself might have been a Catholic church in any small American town, complete with Catholic necessities, idols, and the ever-present money boxes. I gave them a quarter. The holder of holy water, just below the money box, was a large seashell. The priest was busy in the hospital, so we didn't get to see him. His home was a modest, well-kept dwelling with several native boys around it in the process of keeping it up.

Espiritu Santo is an island where one could travel about for a month at least before getting a complete picture of it. I would have liked to have gone up the Sarakata River into the interior, where bananas and pineapples grow wild and the natives grow wilder. Head hunting is said to be a major sport up in those parts, and the travel books say to "treat the inland natives (or bush natives) with extreme caution." As I would sit of an evening and stare at the mile-high peaks with the sun setting beautifully behind them, I would wonder what treasures they held. It seems there must be something up in there just for the taking to make a man rich – maybe diamonds, maybe gold – who knows? No white man has ever been up Santo Peak or Tabwemasana Peak, 6,169 feet high.

One day we set off to go swimming. Up the eastern side of the island are three beaches, one for enlisted men, one for army officers, and one for naval officers. The last was in "Ida Cove" and sold beer and cokes. We went to that one. It was a delightful place, the water warm and the coral sand soft. It was all fixed up with rafts and floats and diving boards, with a checking service and a little café where cold beer and cokes were sold. There were grotesque figures around, which turned out to be men painted all over with gentian violet. A small cut from the living coral that lined the bathing beach would spread through the body, and the fungus growth was very difficult to check. Coming back from the beach, we hitchhiked a ride in a weapons carrier already rather full of officers. We squeezed in on the end seats and floor and started off. Going up a hill, the driver shifted suddenly and let the clutch pedal out fast. The jerk caught Kawula off guard and he landed on his fanny on the road. It was a comical sight, and he was unhurt.

Well, days went by on Espiritu Santo. The cargo was unloaded and a very light cargo put on for our next port. During our stay there we had good radio programs from the American expeditionary station there, giving transcribed programs from the States. Espiritu Santo Island was well set up from a military standpoint and was on a decline from that same standpoint. Units were moving up the line to areas nearer the combat zone. In our travels one day we saw a huge cemetery where were buried some heroes of Guadalcanal, a Japanese general or so, and several U.S. officers who had been unpopular or tyrannical with their men. Front-line justice had taken over.

The day before Easter we were moved out into Segond channel. We sat there all Easter day, unable to get to shore to go to church. Then on Easter night we pulled up the anchor and started for our next port. We left at sunset, and the sun setting behind those towering wooded peaks – behind the blue lagoons separating Santo, Aore, and Malo Islands – was a sight not to be forgotten. Espiritu Santo Island was an experience in life, geography, and tropical beauty which everyone should have. It was a most pleasant port. The parting reminded me so much of a Fitzpatrick travelog: "As the sun slowly sets on Espiritu Santo, jewel of the New Hebrides, we take our leave of this magical island and put out once more into the blue Pacific."

C H A P T E R   1 6

RUSSELL ISLANDS AND GUADALCANAL

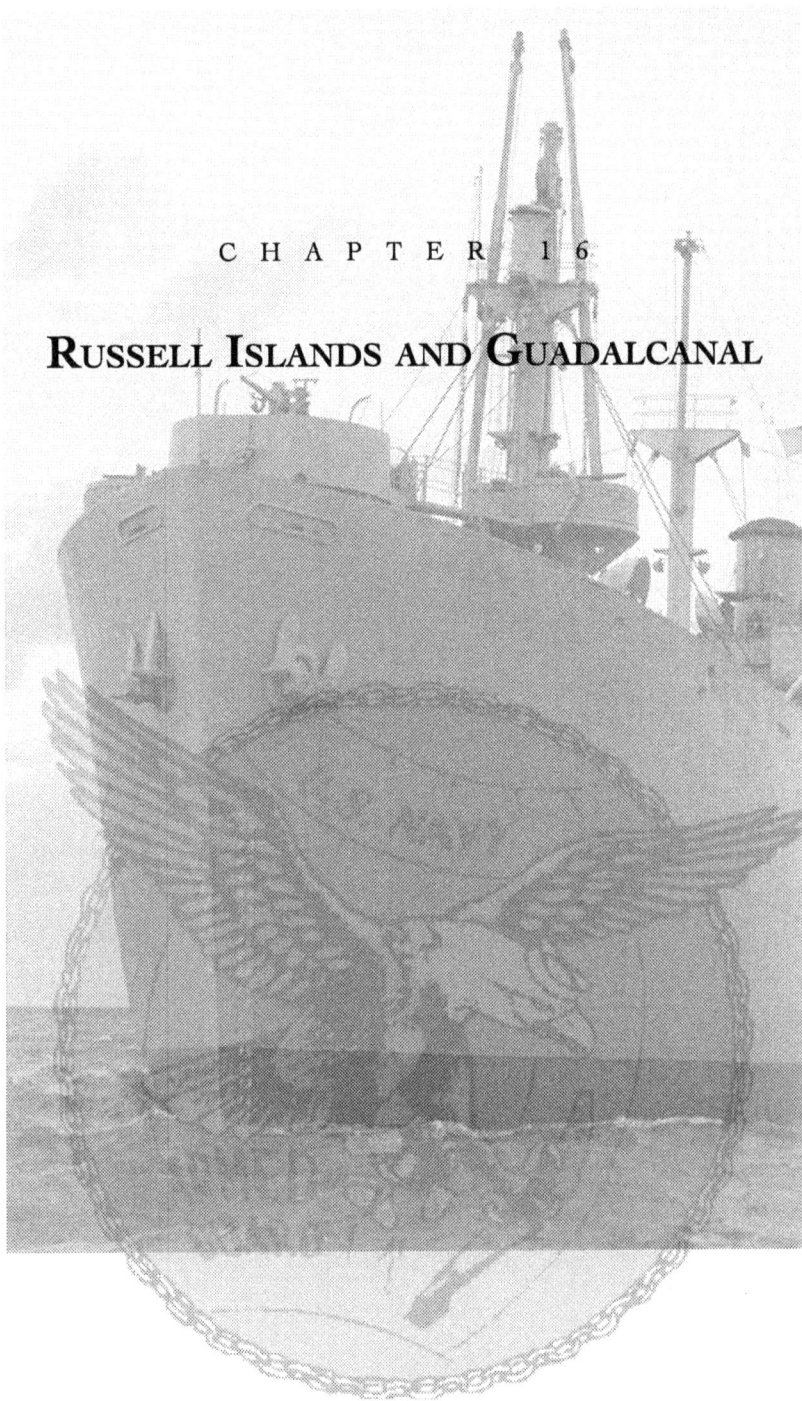

CHAPTER 16

Editor's note: This chapter was written by Asa Casterlin.

We zigzagged our way through a rolling sea to the Russell Islands, a small group of islands within the Solomon Group, just north of Guadalcanal. The morning of April 3rd we went up the "slit," the channel between Guadalcanal Island and Florida Island, scene of great naval battles in the earlier part of this war. Many of our ships were sunk in this section, including the old cruiser *Wilkes-Barre*. Just north of Florida Island is Savo Island, where thousands of marines were lost in taking the worthless pile of lava.

Late afternoon of April 3rd we pulled into the Russell Group. Their beauty paralleled that of Santo Island with the blue lagoons, waving palm trees, and mountainous interiors. Two large and hundreds of small islands make up the group, some of the islands being those one-man affairs pictured in cartoons. The largest island, Pavuvu, has a peak 1600 feet high, and Banika Island goes up 600 feet. These two islands are separated by a narrow passage of water called Sunlight Channel. The Russell Islands are owned and controlled by Great Britain, and the land thereon is leased by Lever Pacific Plantations, Ltd., a subsidiary of the Lever Brothers Company (the soap makers). Practically every square inch of the island is planted thickly with coconut palms, and overseers of the plantations live in little huts dotting the shoreline.

April 4, 1945

We were greeted some distance out by a navy pilot who directed us to "White Beach" (the navy designates their various beaches by colors). At White Beach there were temporary docks made out of pontoons, and we headed for one. The navy pilot, however, didn't do so well (he agreed after that it was only his fifth ship to dock). Our screw hit the edge of the dock, taking a big hunk of brass from the screw and causing much excitement and indignation and speculation as to whether the shaft was out of line. Everything proved to be all right, and the captain finally calmed down. From that time on he docked his own ship and made the pilot take a back seat.

We took on a little cargo at White Beach, then proceeded to Blue Beach, which was around the corner on Banika Island, right at the entrance of Renard Sound. Here we stayed for about three weeks. We took on equipment of the 12th Special Seabee Battalion, consisting of trucks, lumber, oil, and other stuff. At Blue Beach the Red Cross was set up with a recreation room, free coke stand, and canteen. And there were three Red Cross girls – the main attraction. There were also two movies within walking distance and three more within bumming distance. Bumming rides was fairly easy, and it wasn't long before we knew our way around and knew Banika Island like a book.

The movies were strictly open-air affairs, some of the better ones having canvas tops. The officers had a section for themselves, usually elevated and with backs on the benches. On Sundays, church services were held in the movie areas, portable altar and portable organ in place. The Protestant chaplain always preached down-to-earth sermons, and the services were well attended – not approaching the movie attendance, of course, but nonetheless the number coming to church and staying attentive to what was going on was surprising.

On the dock next to ours, something was going on that made Kawula's and my blood run cold. Every day trucks loaded with stuff would come down to unload a one-ton barge. That evening the barge would go out to the center of the channel, and a small bulldozer would push the stuff off into the sea. One day Kawula and I decided to investigate the nature of this unwanted equipment and found on just one barge-load enough radio equipment to keep us both for the rest of our lives. All sorts of scrap metal, pipes, plates, and truck parts were first smashed up and then loaded on the barge for disposal.

The saddest of all was the fine radio equipment from tanks and aircraft. Even large transmitters from permanent installations were first bashed in with an axe and then dumped overboard. Just about this time we were tearing all over Banika trying to get some miscellaneous parts we needed. Fifteen minutes on the junk pile with a screwdriver and we had all we needed. We kept going over and gleaning every day, and before we knew it we both had about 300 dollars worth of radio parts. Some days there would be whole jeeps or trucks on the barge, and one fellow told us there were often new motors still in their crates, but apparently "obsolete," to be pushed over. It seems the stuff belonged to the marines and was expendable, but it all is certainly an argument for centralized supply systems, if not for a centralized military system doing away with the army, navy, marines, and merchant marine.

We got some information about a swimming beach on an island some 45 minutes away and broke out the motorboat one day to investigate. It turned out to be Kurimarau Island, and a perfect place to bathe. A wide coral reef skirted the island, wider than the island itself. The water was delightfully warm, the sand pure white, and the waves small. One could walk out several hundred feet and still not be over one's head. There was no evidence of sharks, as they do not come in such shallow water. The beach teemed with hermit crabs, and we relieved many of them of their shells. Occasionally a band of natives would come to the island to spear fish. They were wild-looking Melanesians with red teeth from chewing betel. They had bushy bleached hair, and each brandished a huge bolo knife for cleaning fish, hacking down coconuts, etc. This one afternoon's catch by 12 natives was over 500 fish. They spread coconut palm leaves on the ground and cleaned the fish in the sea. The natives smoked American briar pipes and wore Sears and Roebuck diving goggles around their necks.

The Russell Islands had not been bothered much by the Japanese, and only an occasional bomb crater reminded one of the war. Our chief mate, Mr. Willie Miers, had acute appendicitis here and had to be operated on at the base hospital. We got to see the hospital by visiting him. It was a dismal-looking place made up very much like post hospitals in the States. The buildings were wood with light steel angles holding up the roofs. They had female nurses and served lots of ice cream to the patients.

The Russell Islands were quite a military installation in their day, but now units were moving out to more advanced areas, and the airstrips were practically deserted. One airstrip was being used for experiments on radio-controlled planes. Each day a cub would come flying over the ship with no one in it, and pretty soon a larger plane (with pilot) would come up to take over control, and the little plane would follow the big one all over. Finally, the field would take control and land the pilotless plane.

Well, finally on April 20th we received our orders to leave for Tulagi and Guadalcanal, where we were to fuel and meet a convoy for Okinawa. We had about 30 seabee enlisted personnel and one officer on board. The seabees were to sleep in the hold on cots. However, they all preferred the main deck.

So, a little reluctant to leave our south-sea island paradise in the one-to-five-dollar-per-day area with the nice beach and movies, we upped anchor and made off for Tulagi, a day's journey. We made Tulagi about nightfall and immediately were surrounded by oil and water barges.

April 21, 1945

Tulagi is on Florida Island, across from Guadalcanal, and

on Purvis Harbor, a deep natural harbor well protected by mountains. In peacetime it is the seat of government for the Solomon Islands. The British government man has a nice house on Pervis Harbor, where it is comparatively cool. The mosquitoes on Tulagi were said to be bad, so we didn't go ashore.

The following day (April 22) we went across the slit to Guadalcanal. We anchored quite a way offshore and took the captain to the port directors in the motorboat. While he was there we stripped and went in bathing to get cooled off. We found that there was "taxi" service between ships in the harbor and the naval advance base, so we spent quite a bit of time ashore.

They had a nice movie house at the naval advance base, and also a barber shop, canteen, Red Cross house, and a PX. The place was quite built up, being near Henderson Field, the main airbase on the island. The second day we started to branch out, having bought all we wanted at the PX, and started to hitchhike up the island. We finally got rides up past Lungi Cove, passing a few native villages and Abla, the peacetime local government settlement.

Finally we came to the camp of the 22nd Marines. The marines live like prisoners compared to naval or army personnel. Their dwellings are only canvas tops, with no floor and no sides. I guess it is to toughen them up.

Near the 22nd Marine base was the Japanese steamship *Kinugawa Maru*, which had been beached, strafed, and burned by the Americans. It was some distance from the shore so we took off our clothes and swam out to it. We had to climb a precariously perched ladder with half its rungs missing to get to the deck. The ship was in pretty bad shape and had been visited many times by souvenir hunters. However, we could see enough to learn that in its day it must have been a pretty nice ship. What we couldn't figure out was the fact that the tops of the bilge-sounding pipes were covered with English directions. Could this be lend-lease? Pre-war lend-lease, I guess. We picked up a few pieces of burnt tile and swam back.

We had only three days at Guadalcanal, but could have used many more there to really see things. A lot of units were moving out from there, although there were still Japanese in the interior. Occasionally they would send a patrol up into the hills to try and root the Japanese out, but usually the patrol never came back. Guadalcanal has high mountains (Mount Popomanasiu being 1,000 feet high) running its entire length, most of which are above the clouds all the time. The Japanese could hide up there and live off the land indefinitely.

One morning, April 25, 1945, we got our convoy of four ships and two escorts and headed for Eniwetok Atoll in the Marshall Islands, a six-day journey. Guadalcanal was to be our last look at civilization for about four months, though we didn't know it at the time.

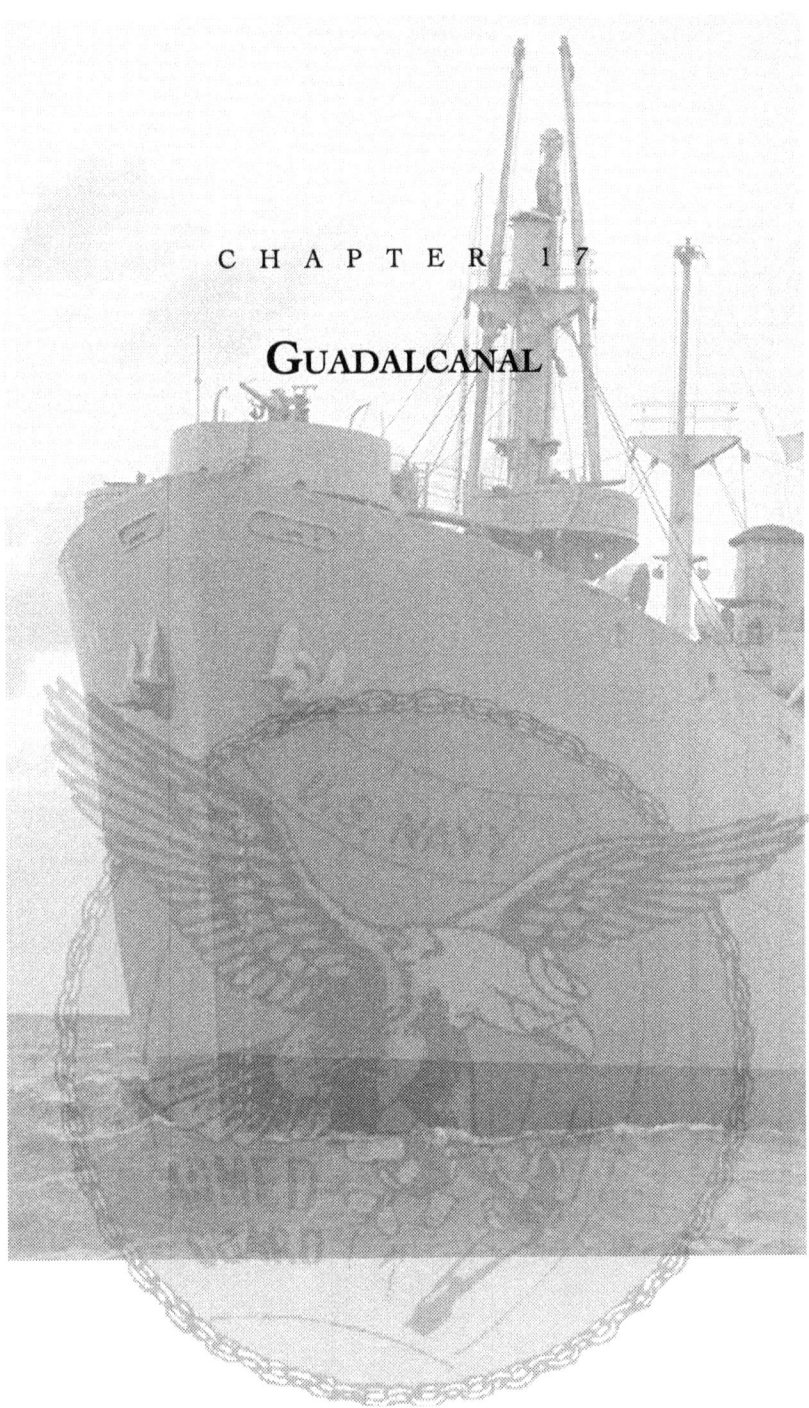

GUADALCANAL

Editor's note: This chapter was written by Henry Valli.

The South Pacific was another scenic wonder, hundreds of small islands. Some have sand, some have lush vegetation. There are coral islands with clear deep blue water. Natives with only a loin cloth and with sticks and bones in their ocher-dyed hair. They had very wide, callused, white-bottomed feet. They never wore shoes. I did not see any women on these islands.

When we arrived in the New Hebrides (Espiritu Santo) we were informed that we were moving north. Even though the gun crew had a lot of sea duty and battle experience, the gunnery officer didn't feel that we were competent, so he got someone from shore in Guadalcanal (Solomon Islands) to train us. How he arrived at the conclusion that we were not competent I do not know, and I will not speculate about his reasoning.

While we were in Guadalcanal he brought aboard a marine gunnery sergeant to show us how to fire the guns. The 3"/50 breech block didn't close fully when the gun was loaded, and we spent quite a lot of time stoning the breech block because it was a tight fit in the breech housing. The training mechanism was also sluggish, but it worked. The marine gunnery sergeant was supposed to fix this problem. When he came on board and saw the 3"/50, he wanted to know how we put the "bullet" in the gun. He told me that he only knew how to use small arms and had never seen guns aboard a ship.

Prior to the sergeant's coming aboard, our gunnery officer wouldn't let me take the training gear apart to see what was wrong with it. He said that I didn't know anything about the training mechanism. He said the problem was with the friction disks and that it was a tricky job to make the proper adjustments. Well, we knew that he was full of crap because friction disks were only on the 5"/38 training mechanism. He had read the manual about the wrong gun. The 3"/50 was a worm-gear drive and probably only needed spacers removed or added to center the worm gear on the ring gear that rotated the gun.

The gunnery sergeant was holding a drift pin, and our gunnery officer was pounding on it, hoping to drive the shaft out of the worm gear. But the worm gear shaft was tapered, and they were driving the shaft in the wrong direction. They managed to crack the bronze bearing that the shaft rotated in. No spare parts were available, so we lived with a gun that was very difficult to train. Finally, when we were ordered in to the battle zone, he became concerned and ordered that the crew be trained and the guns test fired.

There was another incident that occurred when the marine gunnery sergeant was showing us what happens when a 45 caliber pistol jams. We were standing in a circle around him and he was going around the circle showing us what the gun looked like when a jam occurred. When he got around to the gunnery officer, the jam let go and the gun fired at the feet of the officer. The officer was shaken up, and he told me that he made a mistake in not having any confidence in our crew and that the marine gunnery sergeant didn't know anything about guns. He was older than the crew and felt like we were a bunch of kids. We filled out our crew with seabees from Guadalcanal. Some of the merchant crew members were also trained to use the guns. The seabees loaded construction equipment and sailed with us. I don't remember how many seabees we had aboard.

ENIWETOK: A VISIT WITH MY BROTHER

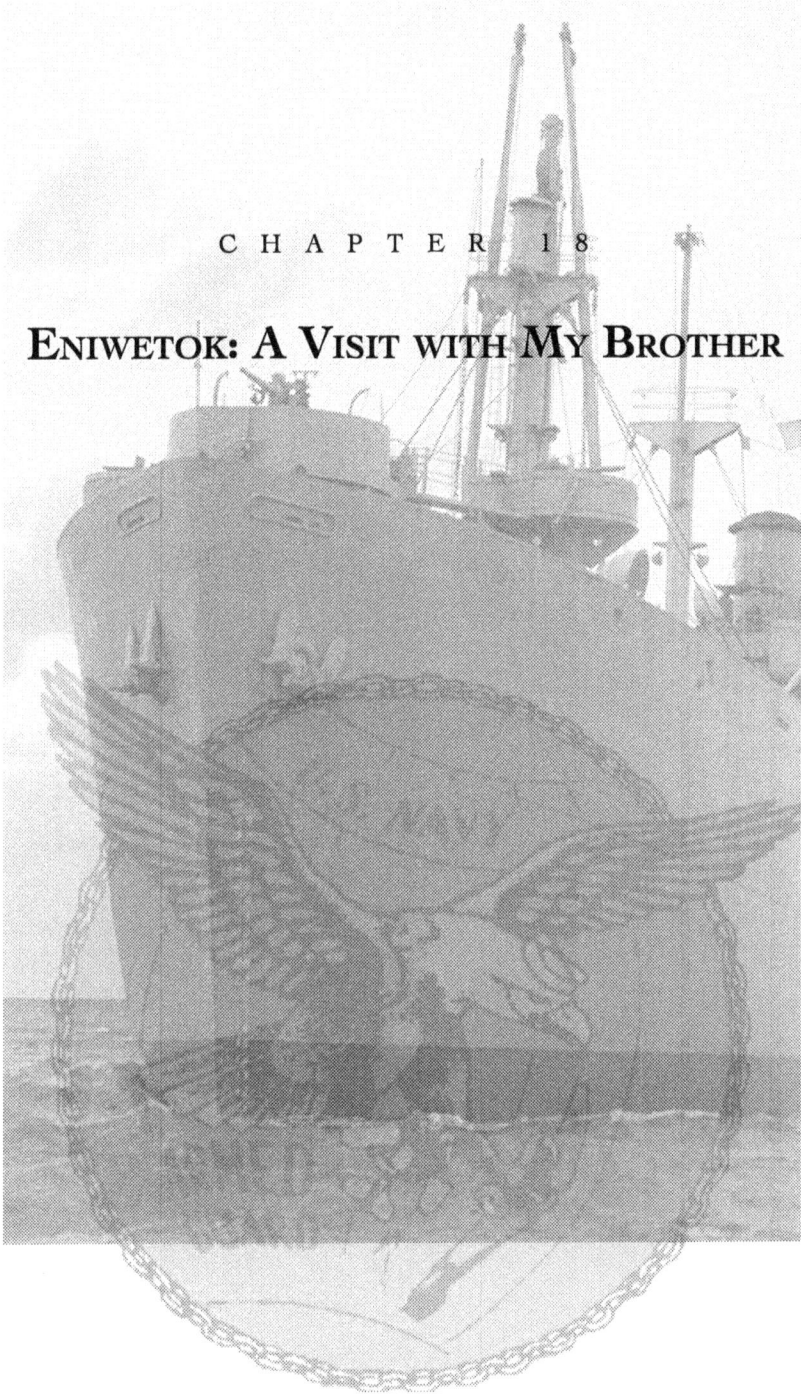

Editor's note: This chapter is excerpted from a postwar letter that John Stockton wrote to Asa Casterlin.

This is a funny story, although at the time it was very scary. I am not sure of the dates, but close enough. I had been in the North Atlantic armed guard aboard a tanker and a liberty ship, including D-Day, since 1943. When I returned to the Brooklyn Armed Guard Center in 1945, I was assigned to the *William B. Allison*, to go to the South Pacific. After many stops at different islands, we went to Eniwetok. After we had anchored I was told by our signalman that DD 652 (the USS *Ingersoll*) was pulling in. He knew I had a brother aboard it. I asked him to ask if my brother was still aboard. The answer was yes, but no information while still underway.

After they had anchored about 600 yards from us, I asked permission to go ashore, pick up my mail, and see my brother. Permission was granted. The merchant crew lowered a whale boat, and Hank Valli and I went over to the destroyer. After all the formalities to get aboard, I was told that my brother Walt was on duty in the engine room. He was a motor mac 2/C, and I had not seen him since he enlisted on December 10, 1941.

When I reached the ladder to the engine room I yelled, "Hey, Stockton, someone wants you up on deck."

He came up the ladder. He had a full growth of beard, and I wasn't sure if it was him. He said, "What the hell are you doing out here?"

I said, "Looking for you."

After talking for over two hours, we were invited to stay for chow at supper time. I mention this because it is an important part of the story. We had beans and wieners. After chow I told my brother where we were going, Okinawa. He said they were going there too for picket boat duty.

I said to him, "See us when you get there and we will get you a meal of roast beef, ham, mashed potatoes, and milk – real milk, not powdered."

We left about four days before he did. But the promised meal would not take place.

CHAPTER 19

ARRIVAL AT OKINAWA

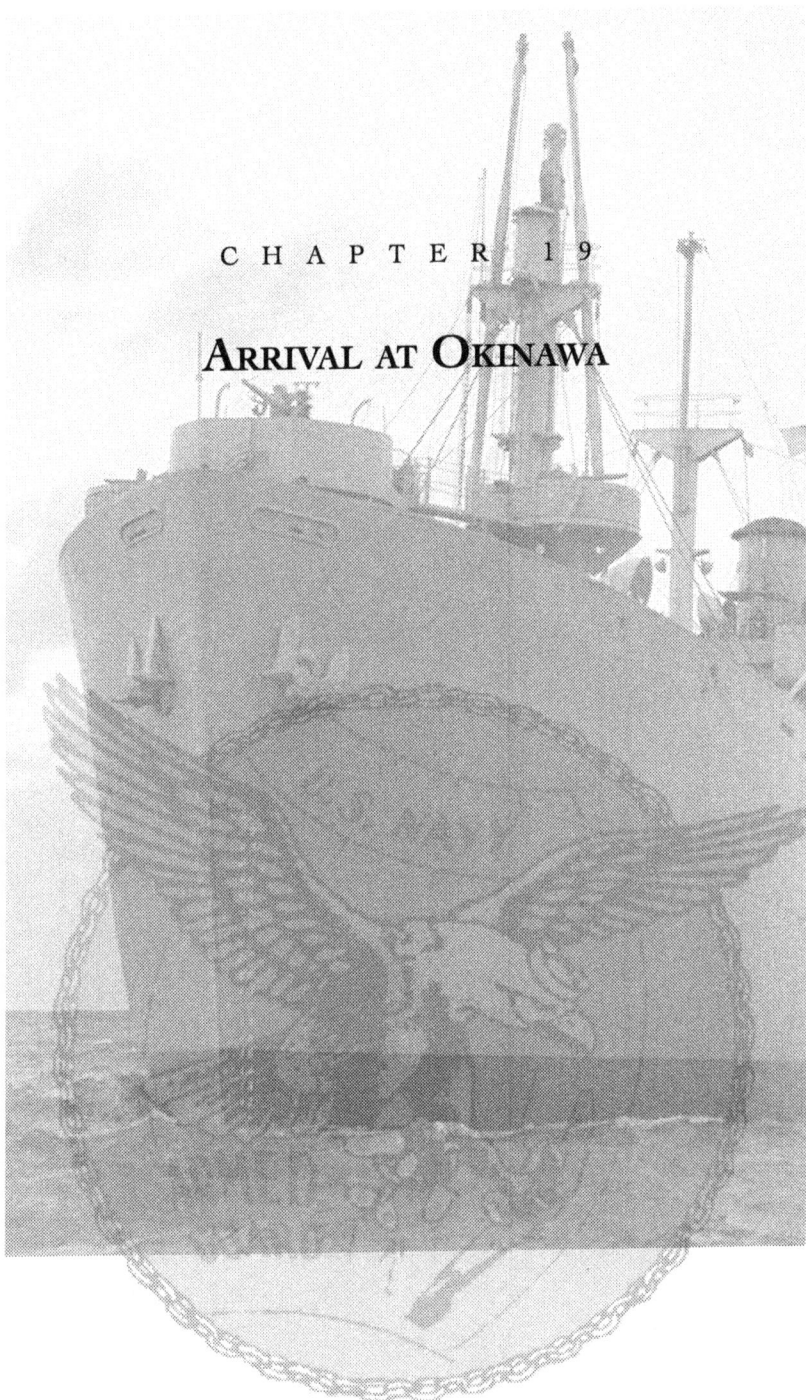

CHAPTER 19

Editor's note: After leaving Eniwetok, the William B. Allison sailed to Ulithi and then on to Okinawa. This chapter is Asa Casterlin's account of arriving at Okinawa.

We left Ulithi on May 15, 1945. From Ulithi Atoll in the Carolines we had an uneventful trip in convoy of five days and six nights. We were escorted by five destroyer escorts, and our convoy was made up of liberty ships, landing ships, and navy supply ships, the AK-94 again taking his place as commodore, with the *Willie B.* as number 53.

We sighted Okinawa Shima early in the morning of the sixth day, May 21, 1945. When we were about 5 miles out of the harbor, we sighted a mine floating a few hundred yards off our starboard bow. Our starboard destroyer escort also sighted the mine and came over and blew it up with fire from their 20 mm guns. The explosion rocked the ship, brought everyone on deck, and gave us a preview of events to come, though we didn't know it at the time.

That morning we went through the nets and entered Nakagusuku Wan, a large bay on the southeastern coast of

Okinawa, just south of Chimu Wan. As we came from the tranquil Pacific into Nakagusuku we had the rude awakening that a war was in progress. Lying in the bay, shelling the southeastern part of the island, were several cruisers, a battle wagon, and numerous destroyers. From the island itself came a continuous rumbling that sounded like thunder but was from gunfire: mortars, machine guns, rifles, and large field pieces. We wished then for the day that we would weigh anchor and get out of there. Our seabees looked mournfully at the shore with its knee-deep mud and absolutely no facilities or barracks and were very sorry the trip had come to an end.

Before we could unload we had to await our turn. Fortunately, we had high priority cargo, comprising stuff needed to set up a seabee camp, and in a couple of days our barges came out to take off cargo. Labor was furnished by seabees, mostly colored, who worked very well considering the difficulties all around them. They ate on the ship out of tin cans.

One of our CPO's went ashore the second day we were in and brought back first-hand stories of the situation on the island. The battle line ran across the island just about opposite where we were anchored, and the fighting was hard. Snipers were always infiltrating behind our lines, sneaking into the various camps with hand grenades and taking lives. Anyone going ashore had to have a steel helmet and a rifle. There was a road across the island, which was of course all mud. The trucks and jeeps were in over the hubs and had to creep along, pushing the mud before them like a snowplow. He also told me how the Negro stevedores were punished if they refused to work or acted up. They would be made to dig up the body of a buried Japanese soldier (they weren't hard to find), dig another hole, and rebury the body. A very unsavory job. The CPO also reported that Naha was a complete ruin. The armies were not even going in to bury their dead, and the stench of the dead could be smelled for miles around.

Nights and days in Nakagusuku Wan were punctuated with air alerts.

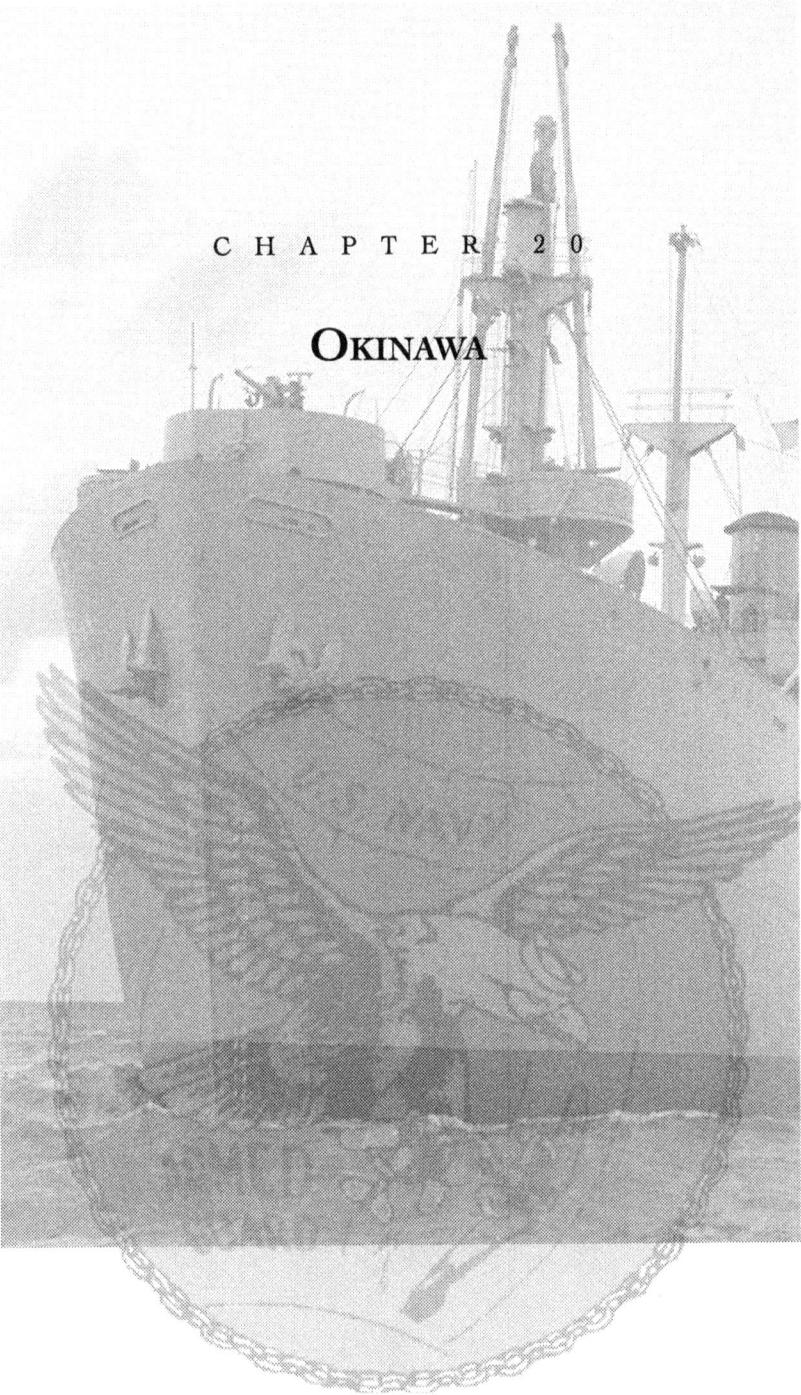

OKINAWA

CHAPTER 20

Editor's note: This chapter was written by Henry Valli.

We waited in Ulithi for a convoy to be assembled and then proceeded to Okinawa. There were ships as far as one could see. When we arrived in Okinawa, the seabees unloaded the supplies on barges before going ashore.

When conditions were declared "Red" we fired our guns at all aircraft. Planes were not supposed to fly over the ships. I remember we fired at a TBF Avenger that was trying to make the shore. He was shot down.

One Sunday morning we were standing on deck, watching a large sea plane running along the shore. Its engine was missing and it was unable to lift off the water. We thought that some marines were fooling around with the plane. The navy supply ship *Hammel* was between us and the shore, and church services were being conducted on the deck. In the meantime, the flying boat finally lifted off the water. We all cheered and clapped our hands. The plane gained altitude, rolled seaward, and crashed into the *Hammel*. I don't know how many casualties there were. The plane crashed into the crowd that was there attending the church service.

It turned out to be a Japanese flying boat that was similar to our PBY.

We fired at kamikaze planes almost every day. One day a kamikaze circled our ship. He was so low that we could see the pilot. Our after 20 mm's were getting hits on the plane. Every fifth round was a tracer shell, and you could see them disappear into the plane behind the pilot. Harris and John Bulluss were getting hits on the plane. The plane was on our starboard side and turned toward our ship, the *William B. Allison*. His left wing clipped the forward 3"/50 gun tub; then the plane spun around and crashed into the ocean. Other ships around were also firing at the plane. The pilot actually survived the crash and was swimming away from our ship. Everyone who had small arms was firing at him. Ships further away from us lowered their guns and fired at him with 20 and 40 mm's. We did not find his body.

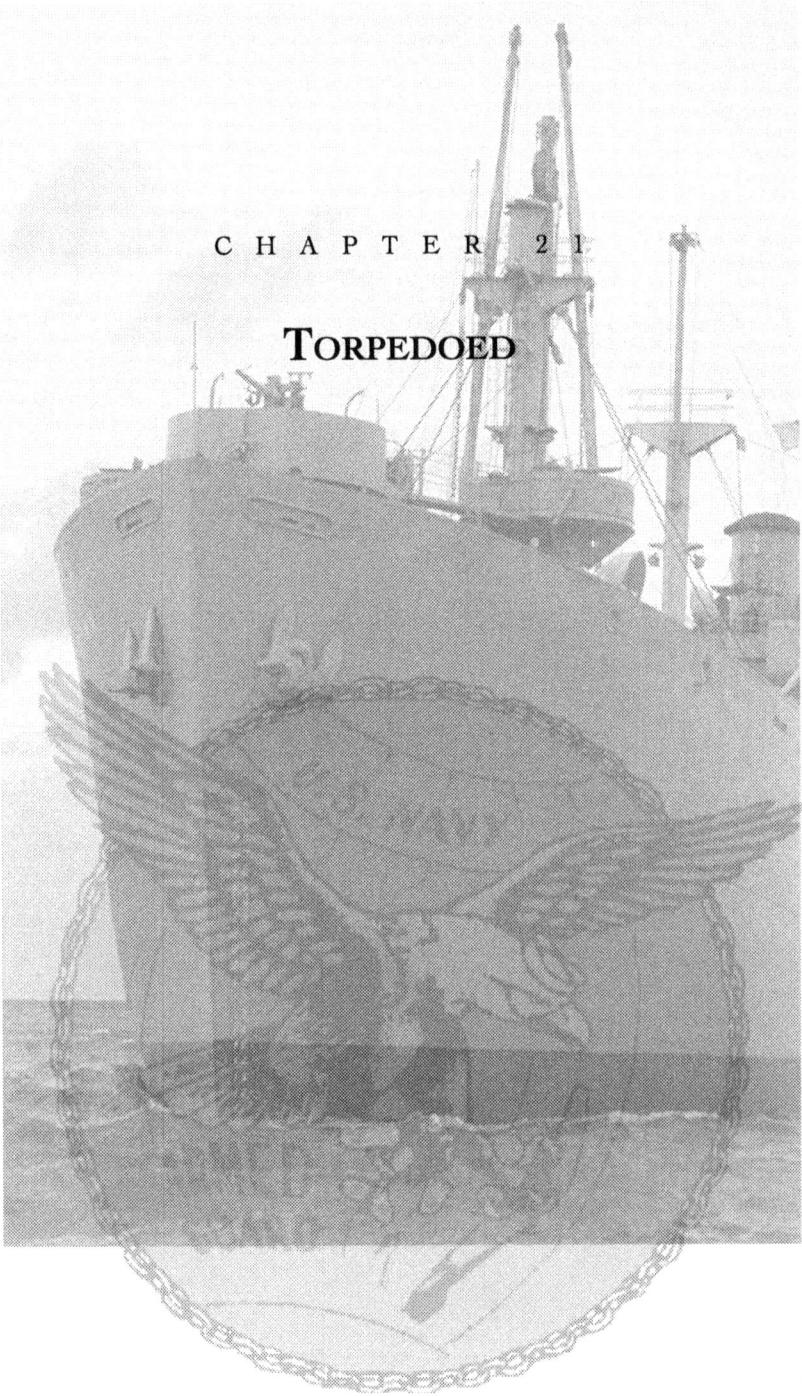

CHAPTER 21

TORPEDOED

CHAPTER   2 1

Editor's note: This chapter begins with John Stockton's account of the
torpedoing of the Willie B.

We arrived at Okinawa and anchored. We were only
there about four hours when we were all awakened by
a tremendous explosion. We had been hit by a Japanese
aerial torpedo.

I remember that after the explosion, when we were on our
battle stations, a kamikaze plane came in over us. He was
attempting to hit us again. We were firing at him. Alongside
us was a navy ship, and he was also shooting. I don't know
if we hit the kamikaze or the navy ship did, but he was hit
and splashed in the water. He survived, and Metcalf, a navy
gunner of our gun crew, tried to kill the pilot with his 20
mm. When swinging the gun around, he hit the boom and
almost cut it in half. By that time the navy gunners blew the
pilot out of the water with their 40 mm.

In the meantime, the battleship (I think it was the *Tennessee*)
was firing their broadside guns at the mountain, and we
would move about three feet each time. We thought we
would break in half. We were doing this while the merchant

men were getting the men out of the engine room. Most were scalded by the hot steam, and we were told that the skin was peeling off their arms as they were being pulled out.

After that, all seemed to get quiet for awhile, but we found out later they all had died.

After resting awhile, with no kamikaze coming, we were all sitting on the deck below one seaman who was sitting in the capstan and who fell asleep. He still had his helmet on, as we all did, but his fell off and hit the deck. We thought we had been hit again and started to run for our battle stations. We were relieved when we realized what had happened. We were really on edge.

We knew when the kamikazes were about to show up. We would see a plane similar to our Piper Cub flying over; we nicknamed him "Washing Machine Charlie."

Editor's note: Hank Valli wrote the following account:

The day before we were hit, May 24, 1945, we were firing our 3"/50 and 5"/38 one round per minute at the Japanese who were holding a heavily wooded area. This was protective fire for our marines who were advancing in that area. We were on a four-hour-on and four-hour-off watch. We fired until we expended all our ammunition. Other ships were also firing into the area where the marines were advancing. It was impossible to get any rest because every time one of the guns fired it would make you jerk all over.

Toward evening there were two destroyers covering us with smoke. We were ordered to suspend all watches so we could get some rest. I was on the after gun deck (5"/38) when the destroyers stopped making smoke and left our area around midnight. At 3 a.m. on May 25, 1945, our ship was hit in the port side, amidship, just above the water line. It had to be a torpedo that never hit the water. The plane just cleared our stack. The ship was painted a light gray and stood out like a sore thumb against the flares that lit up the shore area. The ship's boiler had a full head of steam so that we could get under way immediately if we had to. When the water hit the boilers in the engine room, they exploded. Live steam killed several merchant marines who were in that area. Our gunnery officer, whose quarters were amidship, ended up aft of the ship. He was lying fully clothed in his bunk when the torpedo hit. When I saw him, he just had on his pants and one sock and a shoe. He was completely disoriented.

The ship was low in the water and seemed to be resting on a reef, as the ship did not move with the motion of the sea. To the best of my recollection there was talk of abandoning the ship. When it was determined that we weren't going to sink, the gun crew was invited aboard a mine sweeper for coffee.

We arrived back at the Willie B. as dawn started to break. Harris and I went amidship to look at the damage. A man killed by the live steam lay on the deck.

CHAPTER 22

THE AFTERMATH

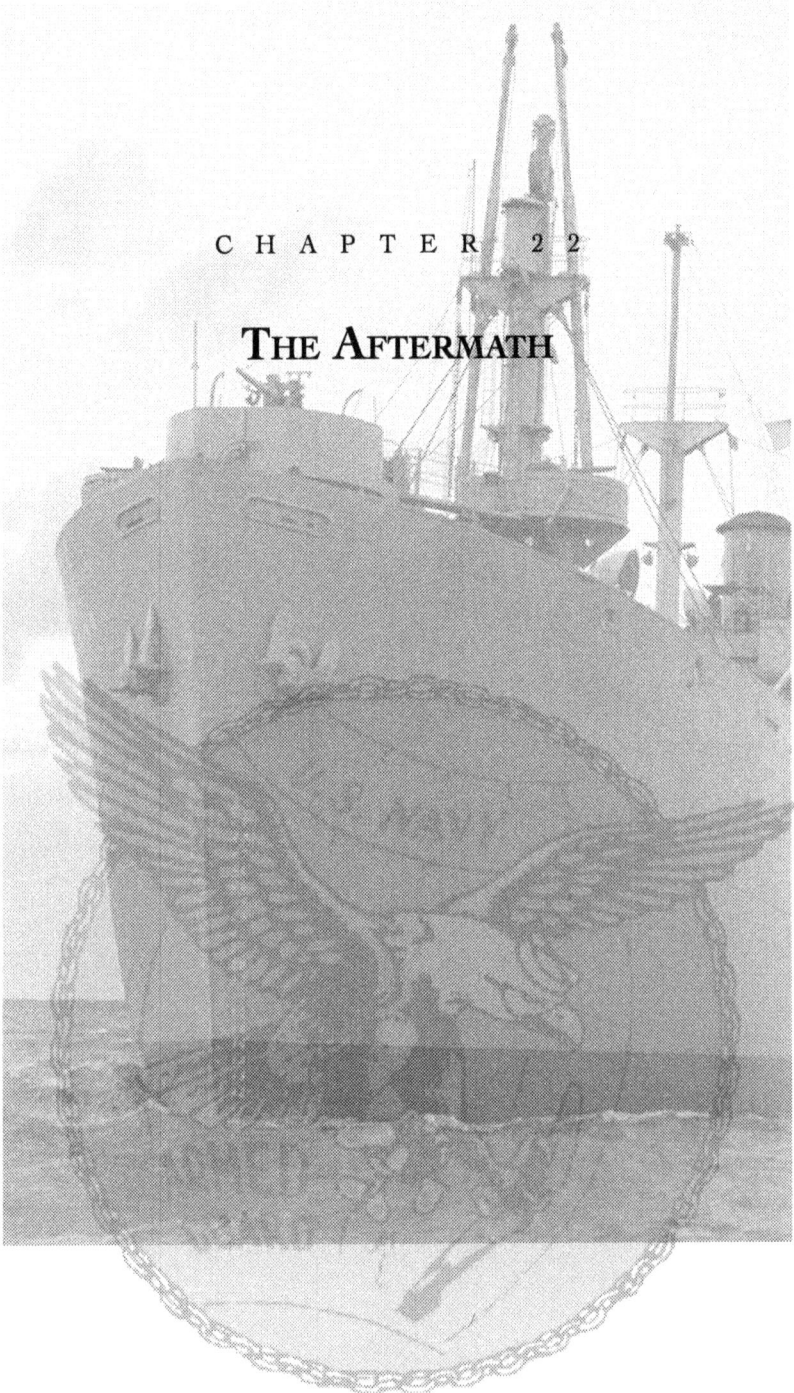

CHAPTER 22

Editor's note: This chapter begins with John Stockton's account of the days and weeks following the torpedo attack.

About two days after we were hit, my brother arrived. He got permission to come over and see me. After looking for me for over one hour, he said to his friend, "We haven't checked the ship with the big hole in it."

He found out it was us when they took their whaleboat and went inside the ship, turned around, and came out to find we were still on board. The first thing he said was, "There goes our good meal." All our stores were in the freezer in the engine room. After we explained what happened, they returned to their ship.

Within five days all the merchant men and our gunnery officer were removed from the ship. Our entire gun crew was left aboard for reasons we never found out. I guess our navy forgot us.

We survived, with the help of the marines on the island, until someone found out we were still aboard. They brought out navy divers, and they welded us together. After unloading the seabees' gear we had delivered, they loaded us up with empty oil drums. We thought now is the time we are going ashore. Wrong. In the middle of the night we were awakened by the sound of people on deck putting tow lines on the ship. We asked where they were going; they said to Kamaretta Bay and that we would be removed in the morning. We said ok and went back to sleep.

In the morning we found ourselves in the middle of a bunch of other ships used for decoys and kamikaze pilots. We had no way to get in touch with anyone ashore to find out what was going on. We were left there for 37 more days. Finally, our signalman and others repaired the signaling lamp, and he kept sending SOS signals to the shore. We could hear gunfire. In the meantime, we were shooting at kamikaze planes.

Later, one day a marine major came out to see where all the shooting was coming from. You should have seen the look on his face when he saw us. He took us back to his barracks, gave us more food, and made arrangements for us to be taken back to the U.S.A.

Editor's note: Hank Valli wrote the following account:

That morning our gunnery officer said he was going ashore to get us reassigned to another ship. The only comment from the crew was that the S.O.B. is crazy. Shortly after that the merchant marine crew was taken off the ship and sent home. Our chow was reduced to C-rations. We bummed these from the marines. Hash and noodles, spam and crackers – they gave us what they didn't like to eat.

The gunnery officer said that he had made arrangements for us to go home. He had packed a trunk and a sea bag, which I was to have shipped to the Armed Guard Center in Brooklyn, and he typed a letter and gave it to me so I wouldn't forget. He left the ship and did not return.

One day a marine major came aboard and said that we couldn't stay aboard because there wasn't any water, food, or electricity. We had been scrounging food, and he wanted to know who the hell we were.

We had ammunition for our 20 mm's and would fire at the kamikaze planes that came within range. We got the bright idea that if we set off a smoke pot when we were attacked, they would think we were hit and go for another ship. If we got lucky and a kamikaze was in range, we could shoot it down. Since the ship was in a fixed position and the wind always seemed to blow toward the bow of the ship, this was the best place to locate the smoke pot. We tied a line on the smoke pot and lowered it into the anchor chain opening. To set it off, it was necessary to pull on a dowel that had a wire attached to the middle of it. You had to grab the dowel with your hand, with the wire between your two fingers, and give it a good jerk. This action detonated the smoke-generating device.

The "condition red" flags went up on other ships. It was time to set off the smoke pot. I couldn't reach the dowel, so two men, each grabbing one of my feet, lowered me into the anchor opening. I gave the detonator a good yank and immediately got a face full of smoke. They jerked me out of the hole. My eyes burned. I couldn't breathe. Everyone scattered, and I tumbled away from the smoke pot. The chain locker hatch was open, and I fell about eight feet into the chain locker. My arms were outstretched, and I landed on my right side with my head hitting my outstretched arm. The air in the chain locker was clear, and I must have been out for about ten minutes. The best that I could do was sit up. The crew came looking for me when the smoke pot started to ease up.

I heard someone say, "He must have fallen overboard."

By then I had recovered enough to call, "I'm down here." They got me out and I ached all over.

I said, "Enough of this shit. If we stay here much longer we'll kill ourselves. Go find the marine major to see when we are scheduled to leave".

Two days later we were aboard the USS *Kittson*, bound for Guam.

AFTERWORD

Thus ends John Stockton's story of his WWII service in the U.S. Naval Armed Guard. There are just a couple of loose ends to wrap up.

After finally being taken off the disabled *William B. Allison*, Stockton was aboard the navy ship USS *Kittson* for a while. He was eventually returned to the U.S. and was discharged from the navy in late 1945.

The *William B. Allison* was declared a complete loss. She was acquired by the navy on July 30, 1945, for use as floating storage for lubricants and other petroleum products at Ulithi. On August 6 she was renamed *Inca* (classification IX-229), but was subsequently renamed *Gamage* (classification IX-227). She was placed out of service on February 8, 1946, and was eventually sold to China Merchants and Engineers, Inc., on February 19, 1948.

Many of the surviving liberty ships served in merchant service after the war, but almost all were eventually scrapped.

Today, only two of the more than 2,700 original liberty ships survive. Fortunately, both have been restored as museum ships that the public can tour and even sail on.

One is the SS *John W. Brown*, docked in Baltimore, Maryland, and maintained by Project Liberty Ship, "a non-profit organization dedicated to the preservation of the liberty ship SS *John W. Brown* as a living memorial to the men and women who built the great liberty fleet and to the merchant seamen and Naval Armed Guard who sailed the ships across the oceans of the world." More information is available online at http://www.liberty-ship.com.

The other surviving liberty ship is the SS *Jeremiah O'Brien*, docked in San Francisco, California. For more information, see http://www.ssjeremiahobrien.com.

Finally, there is also now an extensive web site devoted to information about the armed guard: http://www.armed-guard.com.

From all indications, it looks like John Stockton's "forgotten navy" – the U.S. Naval Armed Guard – will indeed be remembered.

Editor, INTERVIEW YOU

ABOUT THE TYPE

The text in this book was set in a
digitized version of Cochin, a typeface designed by
Parisian copperplate engraver
Charles Nicholas Cochin, 1715-1790.